Arcturus
Star of the Second Coming

Approaching Days of Heavenly Signs and Cosmic Disasters

Daniel Speck

Front cover: Jerusalem at dawn with Arcturus as it might look as a supernova. Author and NASA photos.

ISBN 978-0-7414-1782-4

Published by:

INFINITY
PUBLISHING.COM

1094 New De Haven Street, Suite 100
West Conshohocken, PA 19428-2713
Info@buybooksontheweb.com
www.buybooksontheweb.com
Toll-free (877) BUY BOOK
Local Phone (610) 941-9999
Fax (610) 941-9959

Printed in the United States of America

Published December 2004

Chapters

Introduction

In writing this book, I have attempted to set aside the traditional presumptions about the prophetic Scriptures that most churches hold today, and approach the study of the last days afresh, without preconceived dogmas, as far as that is possible, while firmly adhering to the vital doctrines of the Evangelical faith and the authority of God's Word.

This writing is really more of a personal study than a public statement, but I hope that anyone who finds this publication in their hands will be challenged to confront the impending reality of the Tribulation and the Second Coming of Christ, either for the first time or with a new appreciation. At the least, I hope that the reader will find a few nuggets of valuable information or insight that they can use in their own study of the last days.

I encourage anyone who wants to become familiar with these prophecies to read the Scriptures themselves, starting with Matthew 24 and then the book of Revelation. Also important are Daniel, Zechariah, Joel, Isaiah, Jeremiah, Ezekiel, and II Thessalonians.

Chapter 1

The Brilliant Morning Star

Those things which are the most puzzling to us in the Scriptures sometimes provide the most important clues to a deeper understanding. For instance, the seven churches of Revelation: why did Christ single out these seven churches to give this last important message to? There were many other churches throughout the Mediterranean world, some larger and more prominent.

There are several answers that seem most plausible for this. The first is that the situations of these particular churches fit the pattern of the seven ages of the Church that was to come. No verse of Scripture states this, although the reoccurring phrase, **"Whoever has an ear let him hear what the Spirit says to the churches,"** clearly mark these instructions to be of universal and timeless concern. Revelation is a book about the future and it is in keeping with the purpose of this book that these seven messages to the seven churches are in fact prophesies and guidelines for the church in it's coming centuries.

The following is a chart that represents how these prophecies might have worked themselves out for the past 2,000 years:

EPHESUS: **The Lost Love Church** - 1st Century - New Testament written. Apostolic age ends.

SMYRNA: **The Persecuted Church** - 2nd-4th Centuries - Expansion. Persecution. False doctrines appear.

PERGAMUM: **The Stumbling Church** - 4th-6th Centuries - Roman Empire takes over Church. Orthodoxy established.

THYATIRA: **The Church of Jezebel** - 6th-11th Centuries - Papacy instituted. Paganized traditions and non biblical doctrines prevail.

SARDIS: **The Dead Church** - 11th-16th Centuries - Papal tyranny. Inquisitions. Reformation begins.

PHILADELPHIA: **The Open Door Church** - 16th-21st Centuries - Evangelical Reformation. Global Evangelism.

LAODICEA: **The Lukewarm Church** - 21st Century -Arrogance of wealth. Christ is at the door.

A Graphic Image

Another answer to the question of why these seven churches, we have to stop and look closer at what Christ is telling us in the first chapters of Revelation:

"I saw the seven golden lamp stands and in the center of the lamp stands, One like the Son of man...in His right hand he held seven stars." Revelation 1:12,16.

"As to the mystery of the seven stars that you saw in My right hand, and of the seven golden lamp stands, the seven stars are the seven angels of the seven churches, and the seven lamp stands are the seven churches." Revelation 1:20.

"He who holds the seven stars in his right hand and walks among the seven golden lamp stands..." Revelation 2:1.

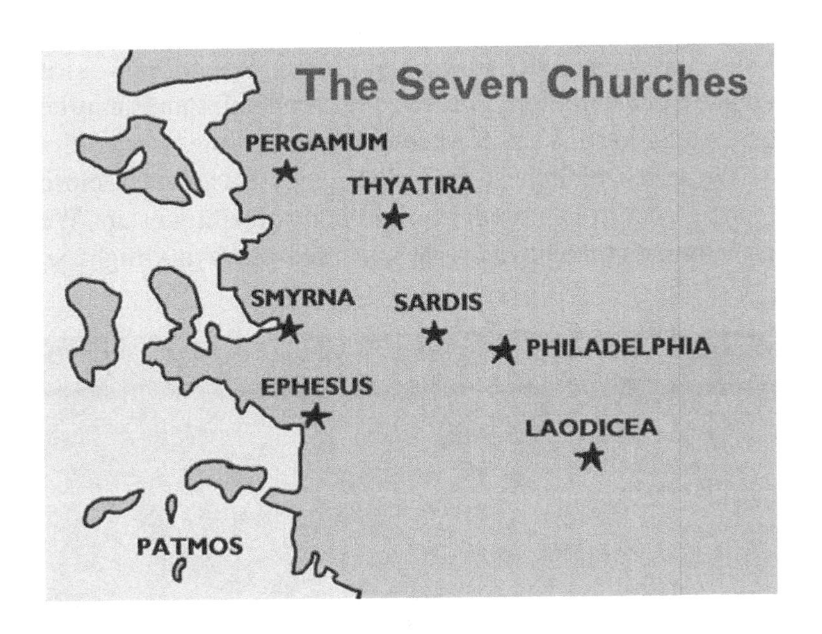

The Seven Churches of Asia

In these first chapters of Revelation, as the Lord shows Himself to John in His heavenly glory, the emphasis He puts on the seven stars and the seven golden lamp stands tells us that they play an important role in the spiritual realities of the universe. The physical universe often reflects what is happening in the invisible heavens. The star of Bethlehem is a good example; it was a stellar harbinger of the most important spiritual event in history.

In the Gospel of Luke, Jesus points out that the physical universe will reflect the realities of the powerful spiritual events of the last days:

"There will also be signs in the sun, moon, and stars...the powers of the heavens will be shaken." Luke 21:25.

Revelation in the stars

Christ walks among the seven golden lamp stands and

holds the seven stars in his right hand. Seven stars is of course a constellation. The seven golden lamp stands may be a constellation as well. If we look at a map of the Greek cities of the seven churches, the pattern they trace has a close resemblance to a particular constellation of familiar stars. We can compare them to the night sky to see where this might be:

Corona Borealis, Bootes, and Arcturus

The constellation of Bootes is very similar. Constellations, being symbolic, need only a vague resemblance to a figure or icon to represent it. In addition to representing the seven churches, Bootes traces the form of a 1st century oil lamp stand. The eight stars of Bootes also look like a fish, the symbol the early Church used for Christianity as we still do today. Traditional astronomy sees Bootes as a herdsman and harvester.

A closer look at Bootes reveals some fascinating similarities to Revelation 2:1, **"He who walks among the seven lamp stands..."** Arcturus is the bright alpha star of this constellation. It is also the brightest star in the northern hemisphere, and the 4th brightest overall in the heavens, but more importantly, it has an unusually fast proper motion. Proper motion is the term astronomers use to describe how some stars have moved over the centuries. Edmund Halley (1718) was the first astronomer to discover that stars move when he compared Arcturus' position with more ancient star charts. Since the 1st century AD, Arcturus has moved 2 degrees in the sky toward the constellation Virgo (the width of two full moons). Only one other star, our closest neighbor, Alpha Centauri, has an apparent faster motion. You could say that Arcturus "walks" among the other stars of Bootes. Bootes is often shown as a constellation of eight stars; Arcturus, the eighth, has been walking among the other seven throughout history. The proper motion of Arcturus might even be seen as the hand of a clock as it sweeps by the seven churches from Ephesus to Laodicea, marking their time off as the centuries pass by.

The other half of Revelation 2:1: **"...and holds the seven stars in His right hand,"** can be visualized when Bootes and Arcturus rise above the eastern horizon before sunrise in the fall. Another constellation, Corona Borealis, is at Arcturus' right hand as it faces us. Corona Borealis is a strikingly beautiful constellation made up of seven bright stars usually described as a crown. They could also be seen as a cup or even a scythe.

The head of Satan

So now we have a picture of Arcturus as it rises in the east. It "walks" among the seven stars of Bootes and has the seven stars of Corona Borealis at its right hand. As we watch it ascend, we notice another constellation just below it. This group of stars is called Serpens Caput, "The Serpent's Head." Most civilizations have imagined this as a snake with its long, undulating line of stars and a triangular head. Serpens has also been called "The Head of Satan." It is a perfect fit as it wriggles at the feet of Arcturus:

Genesis 3:15: **"...(to the serpent) He will crush your head and you will strike His heel."**

Corona Borealis is to the right of, and Serpens Caput is below Arcturus as they rise in the east

The return of Christ will mean the fulfillment of this most ancient of all prophecies.

Star names

Even without the connection with Revelation 2:1, Arcturus might qualify as a harbinger of the second coming solely on its distinctive history. It has one of the oldest continuously used names for any star. It appears in the writing of Homer, Hippocrates, and Ptolemy. It is called Job's star because it is mentioned in the book of Job, the only star mentioned in the King James Bible by name. The name Arcturus comes from the Greek word arktos, which means bear (we get the word "arctic" from it). It is translated as Bear Guard, which is descriptive of its proximity to Ursa Major and Ursa Minor, the Big and Little Bears, or as they are commonly known, the Big and Little Dippers. The Hittites called it "Altaris al sama", arabic for "The Keeper of Heaven." The Chaldeans called it the "Shepherd of the Heavenly Flock." It is invariably associated with some shepherding role in many ancient astronomy beliefs because it "shepherds" or guards the other stars around the North Pole. This is descriptive of Christ as the Good Shepherd of His sheep, the Church.

The Egyptians called it Bau, which means, "The Coming One." This is related to the Hebrew word, bo, "to come," from which Bootes gets its name, thus Bootes also means "The Coming One." The name Bootes could have originally referred just to the star Arcturus, then eventually identifying the entire constellation.

In Greek astrology the constellation Bootes is portrayed as a herdsman with a staff in one hand and scythe in the other; the Shepherd who comes to gather His sheep as well as reap the harvest.

Greek astrology, from which present day astronomy and astrology derives, is based on Babylonian astrology, which comes from earlier Mesopotamian astrology, from which Israel and the Hebrew language arose. The Greeks changed the names of many of the stars and constellations to reflect their own cultural and religious traditions, while keeping the original system largely intact. Ancient peoples did not usually distinguish between astrology and astronomy. The study of the night sky was primarily used in an attempt to foretell the future.

Many of the same names and characters we use today

for the constellations and individual stars go back to the beginning of recorded history, and actually share Hebrew roots. Thus Bo, Hebrew for "To Come," may have been the original name for the star Arcturus.

The Coming One

The "Coming One" identifies Christ throughout the Scriptures. It refers to both His first and second coming. Psalms 118:26 says, **"Blessed is he who comes in the name of the Lord!"**

The prophet Malachi writes, **"...look, He is coming, says the Lord of hosts. But who can endure the day of His coming, and who will be able to stand when He appears?"** Malachi 3:1-2.

John the Baptist asked Jesus, **"Are you the Coming One or should we look for someone else?"** Matthew 11:3.

Revelation begins with John's announcement, **"Behold He is coming in the clouds . . . "** Revelation 1:7.

And finally, the last words of Jesus Himself, **"Yes, I am coming very soon."** Revelation 22:20.

What else would announce the arrival of the Coming One except the Coming One star of the Coming One constellation?

Star of the grape harvest

Mediterranean peoples relied on Arcturus as the star of the grape harvest. It is by this distinction that it is best known in Greek and Roman times. When Arcturus rose as the morning star, it was grape harvesting and wine making time, a significant season in people's lives in the ancient world. Arcturus was prominently associated with the wine cults of

Greek and Roman mythology. If you could ask anyone living in the 1st century Roman Empire which star is the star of the grape harvest, they most certainly would have said Arcturus. A few verses of Scripture:

"(To Christ) Thrust in you scythe and reap, for the harvest time has come, because the earth's harvest is over ripe . . . (to and an angel) Thrust in your sharp scythe, and harvest the clusters of the earth's grape vines, for its grapes are over ripe." Revelation 14:15,18.

"He (Christ) treads the winepress of the furious wrath of God the Almighty." Revelation 19:15.

Planetary progression

A note on Arcturus as the ancient grape harvest star: because of the progression of the celestial sphere over the centuries, caused by a slow "wobble" of the earth's axis (Polaris did not always mark the north pole), the constellation Bootes and the star Arcturus rise later in the fall now than they did in the first century; about a month later in fact. Arcturus rises as the morning star in October today instead of in September as in the first century.

Arcturus, a unique and wonderful star

Arcturus is a stranger to our part of the galaxy. It is a close neighbor, only 36 light years away, but differs from other nearby stars. It is one of the oldest stars associated with our galaxy. It was believed to have formed in the galactic halo, that distant, thin mist of stellar objects that are loosely tied to the Milky Way galaxy. It visits our neighborhood in a wide elliptical orbit much like a comet's. Most scientists think it was formed about 10 billion years ago, twice as long ago as our sun. The universe itself is believed by most astronomers to be no more than 10 to 15 billion years old.

Arcturus is the oldest light in the heavens easily seen with the unaided eye. From ancient times anyone who wanted to look at the oldest object they could see only had to spot Arcturus in the night sky.

It was the first star seen during the daytime with the newly invented telescope. It was observed to dim for a few days in the 1860's, adding to the mystery of its physics. It is believed to have a close companion star, possibly making it a binary.

Arcturus is one of only two nearby stars that are classified as red giants; the other is Betelgeuse in Orion.

The heat falling from Arcturus on the Earth has been measured to be equal to the light from a candle 8 kilometers away.

Some of the statistics of Arcturus:

Diameter: 20 million miles (Sun is one million)
Luminosity: 115 times the Sun
Mass: approximately 1.5 times the Sun
Motion: 2.2 arc seconds per year southeast toward Virgo. In 1 BC it was 2 degrees northeast of today, a little more than two moon widths, one moon width every 820 years.
Temperature today: 4300K (1,200 less than the Sun) and rapidly rising!
Measured over the years:
1920's: 3900K
1960's: 4100K
Type: Red Giant
Visual magnitude: -0.05
Arcturus' companion star: 2.9 AU from Arcturus (1 AU is the distance from the Sun to the Earth)

The rapidly rising temperature of Arcturus is one of its most unique and inexplicable phenomena. It may indicate that something dramatic or catastrophic is about to happen to this star.

Sign of the Son of Man

There is surprisingly little mentioned among Biblical commentators about the sign of the Son of Man of Matthew 24. Few people seem to have any idea what this might be. Most connect it with the next verse of Matthew 24:30, **"And they will see the Son of Man coming on the clouds of heaven with great power and glory,"** saying that Christ coming on the clouds is itself the sign; but there is no point to give a sign if He has obviously already arrived. The purpose of a sign is to signal an impending event or reveal something that may not be obvious. The whole world will know what this sign means:

"Then will the sign of the son of man be seen in the heavens and all the tribes of the world will mourn." Matthew 24:30.

The tribes will mourn before Christ arrives. The sign of the Son of Man would have to be especially spectacular to cause such a universal reaction.

"I AM . . . THE BRILLIANT MORNING STAR"
Revelation 22:16

Arcturus will have to do something unprecedented to become the unmistakable sign of the Son of Man and secure its place as the Brilliant Morning Star. Something like a supernova. A supernova is an exploding star. Supernovas give out almost as much light and energy in their short duration as an entire galaxy. They are usually seen in other galaxies, but a small number have been observed in our own Milky Way. The closest supernova to the Earth in recorded history was some 3,500 light years away. Arcturus is 36 light years from the Earth, almost next door on the galactic scale. A supernova at Arcturus' distance would be the brightest celestial light ever seen in history next to the Sun. Its brightness would be somewhere between the full moon and the sun, turning night into day. It could easily be seen in full daylight. It would probably illuminate the earth with as much light as a heavily overcast day. Brilliant Morning Star would almost be an understatement. It would be a sign that everyone in the world would see, a sign that could not be hidden or mistaken.

The last description that Christ gives us of Himself in His written Word is that He is the Brilliant Morning Star. When He comes again, that may also be the first thing we see of Him; His star shining over the Earth, turning night into day.

In the first chapter of Revelation Christ reveals Himself as the One who walks among the seven lamp stands and holds the seven stars in His right hand. John's description of Him there is also reminiscent of the appearance of a near-earth supernova:

"His face shone as when the sun shines in its full strength." Revelation 1:16.

In the last chapter of Revelation, the Lord tells us that He is the Brilliant Morning Star. He places Himself among the familiar patterns of stars in our night sky. It should be no surprise that we can look up anywhere in the world and behold a symbol of His coming among the same constellations the prophets and apostles were familiar with thousands of years ago.

A Light from the East

Ezekiel tells us that when the Messiah comes the glory of God will come from the east:

"He brought me to the gate looking east and behold the glory of God came from the east. The Sound of His coming was like the sound of many waters and the earth beamed with His glory." Ezekiel 43: 1,2.

In Hebrew this is known as the "Shekinah," God's personal glory. Imagine Arcturus lighting up the sky well before the sun shows itself. It would illuminate the evening sky and replace the sun as the first to rise and create a new dawn.

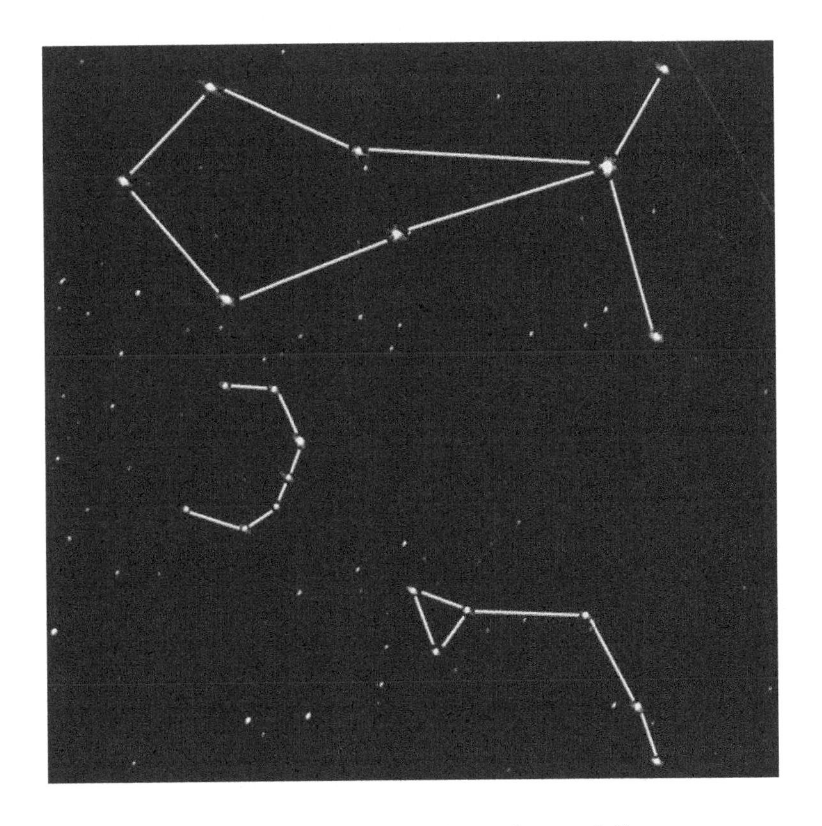

Bootes, Arcturus, Corona Borealis, and Serpens

Follow the Arc to Arcturus

You can find Bootes and Arcturus in the night sky by

looking to the north. Find the Big Dipper, Ursa Major, and follow the arc of its handle down until you come to the first bright star, this is Arcturus. Bootes is the kite-shaped constellation of seven stars around it. Corona Borealis is the U-shaped group of stars northwest of it as it sets in the west or northeast as it rises in the east. In the fall, beginning in early October, Arcturus rises even with the sun on the eastern horizon. Just before sunrise the Big Dipper stands on its tail in the northeast and points southeast to Arcturus. As the month progresses Arcturus rises earlier each day until it can be seen before sunrise in late October, becoming the morning star. The constellation of Serpens Caput lies below and stretches south of Arcturus with its triangular head pointed at the seven stars of Corona Borealis.

On a midwinter morning as the sky begins to pale and all the other stars disappear in the growing light, you can still see the golden point of Arcturus sparkling high in the heavens; the last true star in the northern skies to give way to the rising sun. As the light begins to fade on a summer evening, there is Arcturus again, directly above; the first star to appear and shepherd the constellations around the north pole.

Chapter 2

Supernova Arcturus

According to current scientific theory, there are two main types of supernovas. Type I are supernova that explode when a white dwarf is close enough to a companion star to pull some of its mass into itself so that it expands to a point of more than 1.4 solar masses. This is called the Chandenskar limit. It is that point above which a star can no longer exist in a white dwarf state and by the laws of physics loses its stability, collapses, and explodes, sending a tremendous blast of light and matter out into the universe. There are several main scenarios to create a Type I supernova: a white dwarf that orbits a red giant and pulls some of its inflated mass into itself, or two colliding white dwarf stars.

The other type of supernova is Type II. This comes from a huge star called a supergiant. These are stars that are more than eight solar masses and inflated to many times larger than the Sun. They are relatively young, fast burning stars, that have gone through their stores of hydrogen and helium. All they have left is an iron core which can no longer fuel the star so that gravity suddenly takes over, causing the outer layers to implode and crash into the core, creating a violent "bounce" that then explodes the outer layers into space.

The remains of these exploding stars can be seen in many parts of the night sky in the form of gaseous nebulae expanding at remarkable speeds. They are believed to be the original source of many of the heavier elements like iron and gold. The gold in your ring may have come from a supernova that exploded billions of years ago.

Arcturus' mysterious companion

Arcturus is not believed by most scientists to be a candidate for an impending supernova. Betelgeuse, a nearby supergiant in the constellation Orion, is believed to be a better candidate to explode soon. Arcturus would be a surprise if it exploded. It has some of the elements to qualify it for a potential supernova, and not others. It would probably have to be a type I supernova, because it is not massive enough to explode as a type II. Arcturus would probably need a white dwarf orbiting it that would actually become the supernova. Little is known about its companion star. There even seems to be disagreement among scientists whether there is a companion star at all. The Hippocurs Satellite that studies and classifies stars has detected evidence that it has a companion and so lists Arcturus as a binary star. Other studies of it have concluded that it is not a double star. It may be an optical double. An optical double are two stars very far apart that look close because they are along the same line of sight.

Future scientific revelations

The science of astrophysics is an ever-changing study. With more powerful tools, like the Hubble Space Telescope, we are learning something new about the cosmos almost every day. Astounding surprises in the heavens are being revealed on a regular basis. Phenomena that alter our current understanding of physics and cosmology are continuously being reveled to scientists. Theories about how supernovas occur and which stars are most likely to explode are still being revised. More study is almost certain to expand our knowledge of these spectacular blasts, the most violent events in the universe.

Recently, the new, intensive studies of supernova have reveled new information on how and why supernovas explode. Some well-established theories may have to be changed to fit this new harvest of information. Stars that do not exactly fit the current pattern of potential supernovas may become prime candidates in the future.

Eta Carinae, a massive star and a gamma ray burst source surrounded by a spectacular nebula, is believed to be a prime candidate to explode as a supernova at any time. At 8,000 light years away it would pose no danger to the Earth. NASA

Waiting 36 years

It is important to note that Arcturus is about 36 light years away, the length of a human generation. This is the time it takes individuals to reach maturity and then raise their own child to maturity, completing the cycle of life. Matthew 1 divides the history of Israel into three eras of 14 generations: from Abraham to David, from David to the Babylonian exile, and from the Babylonian exile to Christ. Each of these eras is about 500 years long (except Abraham to David). Fourteen generations of 36 years is 504 years.

Thirty-six is also a multiple of 12, which is the number the Scriptures use to designate human regeneration. The 12 tribes of Israel, the 12 Apostles, and the 12 periods of a woman's fertility each year are all examples. The heavens reflect this number in the 12 phases of the moon each year as well as the 12 constellations of ancient astronomy. If Arcturus explodes into a supernova it will be about a generation, 36 years, before we see it here on earth. Christ tells us about the events of the last days:

"I assure you that all this will happen before this generation passes away," (Luke 21:3) - suggesting that the events of the last days will all occur within a single generation.

On its way?

If Arcturus exploded into a supernova, we would not know about it for 36 years, the time it would take for the light to reach the earth. The vast distances of the universe means that it might have already occurred and its brilliant light may be on its way to earth even as you are reading this.

Coming on the clouds

"If they say to you, 'he is out in the desert, do not go out,

if they say to you, 'he is in these rooms here', do not go, for as the lightning flashes in the east and is seen in the west so will the coming of the Son of Man be." Luke 18:23,24.

This statement is given by Christ to distinguish His coming from the many false prophets that will infest the last days. John tells us in Revelation:

"Behold He is coming on the clouds and every eye, even of those who pierced Him, will see Him." Revelation 1:7.

Christ is prophesied to come as He left, on the clouds. Most likely white, atmospheric clouds, but supernovas produce nebulas, stellar clouds - colorful, luminous gases that expand at tremendous speeds. The supernova that created the Crab Nebula can easily be seen with a pair of binoculars. Shortly after a supernova explosion of Arcturus, a massive stellar cloud would begin to spread across space and would eventually be visible to anyone on earth. The entire planet might see a colorful, glowing cloud as a glorious backdrop for the returning Messiah. There are thin clouds of gas in many parts of the galaxy that are invisible because there is no nearby light to illuminate them. When a supernova occurs, its brilliant light bounces off any galactic nebula in its nearby vicinity, causing them to reveal themselves in a sometimes spectacular glow. If it is near our solar system, this illumination may stretch across the night sky, transforming it into clouds of dazzling colors. The massive shower of radiation could also create an unprecedented light show at the Earth's poles, creating a super aurora borealis.

A flash like lightning

There is still another clue in Matthew 24 that a brilliant supernova will signal the coming of Christ:

"For like the lightning that flashes (comes out) from the east and shines in the west, so will the coming of the Son of Man be." Matthew 24:27.

We can accept this verse as describing the nature of the Second Coming: in the heavens and visible to the entire world; but it also describes the direction, just as Ezekiel says, from the east. It fits a description of an Arcturus supernova coming out of the east as it rises in the morning and shines westward over the planet. It also describes the suddenness of a supernova explosion. It is not a slow, but a sudden event, like lightning. Astronomers have yet to capture the first minutes of a supernova because they appear so suddenly, almost instantaneously.

The days of heavenly signs

The Lord tells us the powers of the heavens will be shaken in the catastrophes of the Final Period. The last days of history will be punctuated by dramatic events from space never before seen or imagined. Not since the Magi who followed the star of Bethlehem will an understanding of astronomy and its connection with the prophetic Scriptures be so important.

Chapter 3

The Supernova and the Seven Bowls

The Seven Golden Bowls of God's Wrath in Revelation 15 begins as one of the four living creatures hands the seven angels seven golden bowls full of the wrath of God. These four living creatures, the eagle, the bull, the lion, and the man, represent the creation as four is the number the Scripture uses to signify the creation. We can reason from this that the seven bowls of God's wrath have primarily a natural cause, since they originate from one of these four living creatures.

"Then one of the four living creatures handed the seven angels seven golden bowls full of the wrath of God . . . 'Go your way and pour out on the earth the seven bowls of God's wrath.'" Revelation 15:7 and Revelation 16:1.

"The fourth angel poured out his bowl on the sun and it was permitted to scorch humanity with heat. People were scorched with terrible heat and they blasphemed the name of God, who has control over these plagues." Revelation 16:8,9.

These golden bowls are "poured out" directly on: the earth, the sea, the rivers, the sun, the throne of the Beast, the Euphrates river, and the air. This sounds like a detailed description of how the flood of radiation from a nearby exploding star would pour into our solar system and ravage our planet.

One other detail: Arcturus is a yellow-orange colored star, a golden star.

When we examine the four golden bowls, they have a similarity to the plagues that God struck Egypt with during the Exodus. This is appropriate because the Egyptian plagues were used to free the Jews from Pharaoh, just as these future plagues will be used to free mankind from the last and worst pharaoh, the Antichrist.

In short, the seven plagues are:

1. Malignant ulcers
2. The sea turning to blood
3. The rivers turning to blood
4. A scorching sun and painful darkness
5. Drying up of the Euphrates River
6. A terrific storm and the most severe earthquake in history.

Most, if not all of these, could be caused by a nearby supernova. As Arcturus exploded, it would send a stream of energy and matter out into the universe on a collision course with our solar system. The energy from this explosion, like visible light, x-rays, and neutrinos would shower the earth at the speed of light, 36 years after the event. It would also create a subsequent wave of super lightweight particles traveling at nearly the speed of light that would impact our planet shortly after. As this wave entered our atmosphere, it would interact with the atoms in the air, converting some of the radiation's energy into mass, creating an atmospheric shock wave that would shake the entire planet.

Just as the earth would be bombarded with this energy, the sun would be flooded as well. One scientific theory states that a neutrino flux from a nearby supernova would heat up the sun. This is exactly what would happen during the third bowl of God's wrath, the sun scorching the earth with its heat. The resulting storms on the sun could change its color and temperature and wreck havoc with the earth's weather. A dense cover of clouds over the earth might result which could then plunge the world into freezing darkness.

A wave of low mass particles traveling near the speed of light could quickly follow, hitting the earth like a hammer. Earthquakes like none ever experienced in human history would shake the entire globe, leveling cities and forcing tremendous geological changes all over the world.

"...a tremendous earthquake as had never occurred since man existed on the earth, so extensive and severe was it. The great city split into three parts and the cities of the nations fell." Revelation 16:19.

"...and the Mount of Olives shall be split in the middle eastward and westward by a very great valley . . ." Zechariah 14:4.

The prophet Zechariah also describes the dramatic meteorological and geological changes that will accompany the coming of the Messiah:

"In that day there shall be no light, but cold and freezing. It will be a unique day known to the Lord, neither day nor night, but at evening time there will be light. In that day living waters shall flow out from Jerusalem, half to the former sea and half of them to the latter sea . . . " Zechariah 14:6-8.

As Zechariah mentions here, **" . . . at evening time there will be light."** Light in the evening, not during the day? The familiar day-night cycle seems to be turned on its head, at least for a time. Arcturus could be that source of illumination that replaces the darkened sun as the light from its brilliant burst shines over the planet before the sun rises.

The sun itself may actually be dimmed by a vast wave of radiation and particles that interfere with the way it normally functions, as the Scriptures say, **"to the color of sackcloth."** It is usually assumed that a darkened sun would be caused by debris and smoke in the Earth's atmosphere that would make it only appear to have dimmed. But the sun itself could turn dark as a natural occurrence, accompanied by a moon of blood-red color that reflects the altered state of sun, as the surface of the sun cools and changes color. When a star like our sun cools, its appearance changes from yellow to orange to red and finally to a dim, dark red. If this scenario occurred, the brightest light in the heavens, even during the day, could actually be the Arcturus supernova!

The dark red sun would reflect off the surface of the oceans and other bodies of water, creating the illusion of oceans and rivers of blood. A "supernova winter" would result, as much of the light and radiation from the sun are temporally cut off. The earth's weather would certainly be radically altered as never before in history. The seventh seal brings storms, earthquakes, and a plague of huge hailstones:

"Hailstones, as big as hundredweights, fell down from the sky upon the people. And the people blasphemed God for the plague of hail, because it was so fearful." Revelation 16:21.

Those prophecies in the Scriptures that seemed to be wild exaggerations or strictly miraculous may in fact be physically possible within our current understanding of science and physics.

The seven bowls

The first bowl, the plague of malignant ulcers would

be easy to connect with a nearby supernova. A vast, unprecedented stream of energy would pass through our atmosphere and affect anyone with their skin exposed. Malignant skin cancer, as most people know, is usually caused by overexposure to radiation from the sun. Radiation falling from a supernova would likely destroy part of our planet's ozone layer to allow the dangerous radiation that is normally filtered out to reach the ground. These ulcers are described as malignant. Malignant cancer is one of the deadliest and hardest to cancers to cure. If a nearby supernova occurred, it would appear suddenly in the sky, catching anyone outdoors by surprise with a massive dose of radiation. Before the danger was realized, many people would be unaware that they had absorbed large amounts of harmful x-rays and gamma rays. Like getting caught in a nuclear blast, radiation burns and skin cancer would be reminiscent of the horrors of the Hiroshima bomb.

Rivers of blood

The second and third bowls cause the seas and rivers to turn to blood. These are the most difficult plagues to attribute to a supernova, but the great flood of radiation and exotic particles could undoubtedly wreck havoc with the marine life that lives in waters of our planet. With the world's ecological balance destroyed, perhaps some types of algae, plankton, or bacteria would multiply so rapidly that the seas and rivers would turn blood red. The massive flood of radiation from the blast might also induce the wild growth of such organisms. The early years of atomic testing showed us that plants exposed to certain types of radiation could experience genetic mutations and massive, unnatural growth. In the 1950's Hollywood made a handful of "B" horror movies based on this premise.

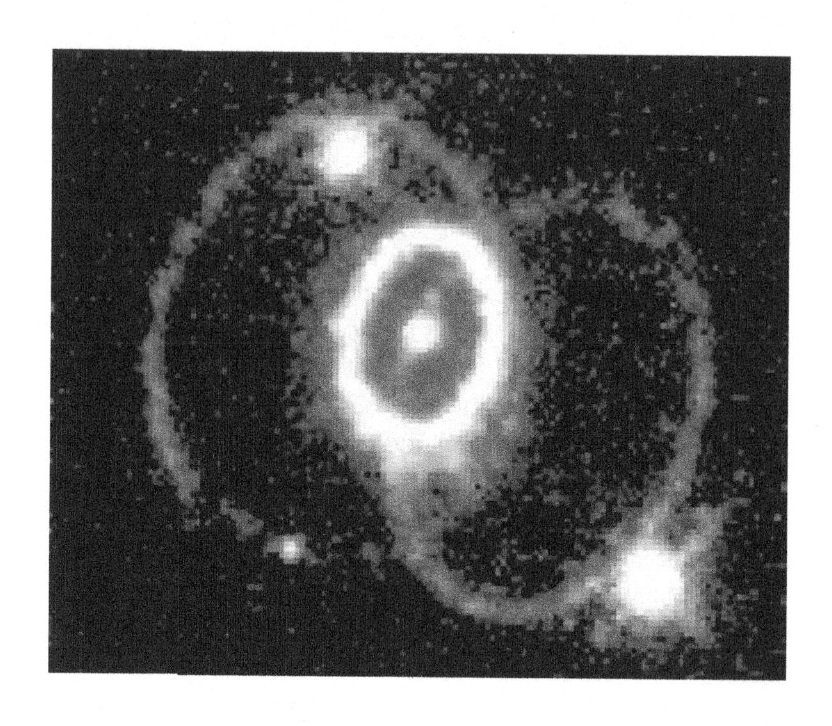

The expanding shock waves of the 1987 Supernova. NASA

Impact on our cosmic neighborhood

The effect of a supernova on the rest of the solar system and other nearby star/planetary systems would be tremendous. Supernovas are believed to have a role in planetary birth. The concussion of the expanding energy and matter from an exploding star can serve as a compressor of interstellar gas and rock to force the formation of whole star/planetary systems. One theory states that our solar system was pushed into forming its present state by just such a shock wave from a nearby supernova.

The more scientists study supernovas, the more they realize that these events are crucial to many of the processes that create so much of the variety of elements, molecules, and structures that makes up everything that is in our galaxy. Supernovas are like cosmic hammers that forge the stars, planets, and elements into an abundance of special substances and structures needed to make a complex planet of life like ours possible. Supernovas truly shake up the heavens. What are the effects to the stars and gases around them? Astronomers are just beginning to find out.

If Arcturus explodes some of its nearby companion stars, even nearer to it than our sun, will be changed in ways that we can only guess at. Christ emphasizes that, **"the powers of the heavens will be shaken**." This will prove to be no exaggeration if a massive shock wave of radiation and particles speeds out into space in our galactic neighborhood. Many of the stars we have looked at for thousands of years may be changed before our eyes. The other bodies of our solar system may also feel the effects of this blast, possibly throwing moons, asteroids, and comets out of their familiar orbits. The planets, including our own could experience atmospheric and geological disturbances that induce permanent changes in how entire worlds look and function. This stellar tsunami may change the ecology of our earth and the appearance of our solar system forever; perhaps even ravage many of our nearby stars.

Chapter 4

The History of Supernovas

A supernova in a spiral galaxy showing the relative brightness of this single star to an entire galaxy of billions of stars. NASA

Supernovas have become one of the most commonly observed events in the universe. We can see them exploding in many of the distant galaxies observable from earth. They go unnoticed by the general population because they are so far away and faint that they can only be seen through a telescope. With the orbiting Hubble Space Telescope and other newer, powerful earth-based telescopes, we can watch supernovas occur more frequently and clearly than ever before. They are really a natural part of the events that happen within all galaxies. However, they do not show themselves very often in our own galaxy during the span of a human lifetime. The estimates for a supernova event within a single galaxy like ours is about once every 100 years. So why have only a few been seen and recorded throughout history? The answer is that there is so much gas and interstellar material obscuring what goes on in the rest of the Milky Way that we see just a fraction of these bright events. We are looking at our home galaxy edge-on. From the Earth we can see almost nothing that happens on the other sides. They are actually easier to observe in other galaxies, especially when we can see the spiral arms as if directly from above, where clouds of galactic material cannot hide them.

Supernovas in history

Nova means new. Many astronomers in the ancient civilizations of Europe, Asia, Africa, and the Americas recorded these new stars. Supernovas bright enough to be seen without a telescope have occurred only a small number of times in human history. In 1006 AD the brightest supernova ever seen was recorded by monks in Europe and by astronomers in China. Other known supernovas have occurred in 185, 393, 1054, 1181, 1572, and 1602 AD. The 1054 supernova is believed to have produced the crab nebula, one of the most visible and most photographed nebulas in the night sky.

Bethlehem star a supernova?

In 5 BC, close to the estimated time of Christ's birth, a bright star, either a supernova or a comet, was recorded by the Chinese. A Syrian coin from the first century depicts the constellation Aires the Ram (the Ram may be a symbol of Israel) with a bright star to its right, possibly showing this same supernova. Speculations about these records being associated with the star of Bethlehem are intriguing but not conclusive. The description that Matthew gives of the star moving ahead of the Magi south from Jerusalem then coming to rest over Bethlehem does not precisely fit any cosmic phenomena we know of, but of the cosmic events that we are familiar with, a supernova is the most likely. A comet would probably not be rare enough to qualify and a conjunction of planets would be much too common as well, to be the sign of the most important event in history. The fact remains that Christ's first coming was heralded by an unusually bright star of some kind, so it is logical to assume that His second coming will be announced in a similar way.

The Magi, the eastern astrologers and astronomers, who followed the star to Bethlehem, were familiar enough with stellar events as well as with the Jewish Prophets like Daniel (from the Babylonian captivity) that they knew that such an unusual and spectacular star in a certain part of the sky could only mean one thing; the Jewish King, the Messiah, was about to be born.

It is interesting to note that the star of Bethlehem also seemed to "walk," and did not simply lead the Magi in a straight line, but may have moved south from Jerusalem after leading them from the east. It is described as having "**. . . rested above the place where the young Child was.**" Matthew 2:9.

These descriptions may note the actual movements of the star or just the perceptions of how it seemed to behave. The Magi may have turned off their course of following the direction of the star as they entered Jerusalem, then took up their course again when they left the city. The star may have dimmed in brightness as they reached the place where the

Christ child was staying. They might have interpreted this as the star "resting" over the place.

The Bethlehem star was seen in the west as the Magi traveled from the east, the opposite of Arcturus as it rises above the eastern horizon in the fall. Aires is on the opposite side of the sky from Bootes. The two stars and two constellations that may represent the Messiah's two coming are the two halves of God's perfect plan. Like two sides of a coin, different, but writing a completed story.

A 1st century Syrian coin depicting the constellation Aires and a special star. The Star of Bethlehem as a supernova? From the Molnar Collection

The latest supernova visible to the naked eye

In 1987 a supernova exploded just outside our Milky Way in the Large Magellanic Cloud, a close neighboring galaxy. A wave of neutrinos from the blast was recorded in several underground neutrino detectors days before the nova was seen visually. These detectors are large, elaborate tanks of liquid far below the surface of the earth that have arrays of sensitive detectors which flash as they catch the rare collisions of these exotic particles with chlorine atoms. This supernova was the brightest seen in modern times. Although it happened outside our galaxy at 160,000 light years away, it was easily visible to the naked eye from the southern hemisphere.

What happens when a supernova explodes

When a Type I or Type II supernovas explode, neutrinos, strange particles that are believed to have no mass but carry energy, explode into space first. They are forerunners of the coming event that will soon be visible. They travel at the speed of light and are so tiny that most pass right through our planet as it if wasn't there. The visible light and radiation such as gamma rays and x-rays follow. The mass of the star then streams out into the universe at 10,000 to 40,000 kilometers per second. Within a day the supernova is a brilliant ball of white light a billion miles in diameter that will eventually be seen millions of light years away in distant galaxies. After several days the expanding ball of brilliant matter begins to thin and cool. As it cools it changes color and shifts to the red end of the light spectrum. As the gases continue to cool and the supernova starts to dim, it leaves behind an expanding, glowing cloud of gas and debris speeding out into the universe, full of complex matter that seeds the heavens with heavy elements. Type I supernovas then leave behind a small, dense neutron star at the center of this expanding cloud.

The "half life" of most Type I supernovas is about 50 days, that is, it usually takes that long for the nova to dim to half of its fullest brightness, dropping off steadily from there until it is no longer visible. Historical records show that supernovas have been visible to the naked eye from a few months to a few years, the average being about 10 months in duration. The great supernova of 1006 was visible for almost two years.

The energy carried off by invisible neutrinos

represents about 99% of the energy that comes from a supernova. The light we see represents only about 1% of the energy of the blast. The gamma rays and x-rays that spread out into the surrounding space are so lethal that they are a major concern of space programs, especially for long-term missions such as a voyage to Mars. Our solar system is continually being bombarded with hazardous x-rays and gamma rays from distant supernovas. We on Earth are relatively safe from these constant streams of radiation because they are largely deflected by our planet's magnetic field and blocked out by our atmosphere. We get some of this lethal radiation from the sun, but the great majority of it comes from exploding stars inside and outside our home galaxy.

Has a nearby supernova already changed our planet?

Discovery of an abundance of a radioactive isotope, iron-60, in deep-sea sediments have led scientists to believe that a nearby star exploded into a supernova about five million years ago and led to a mini extinction during the Cenozoic Era. These isotopes have no known earthly cause and so it is theorized that they are the radioactive ashes of a supernova about 100 light years from Earth. The effect of this nearby explosion was believed to have caused a sudden increase in cloud cover leading to an artificial winter and a dramatic decrease in the ozone layer by the formation of nitric oxide in the stratosphere.

Other scientists have found elevated levels of carbon-14 (the marker used by archeologists for radiocarbon dating) in an underwater cave in the Bahamas that most likely came from supernova radiation. Radio carbon-14 comes only from cosmic radiation. The elevated levels there show a peak at about 44,300 years ago, leading them to suspect that one of the ice ages was a result of this increased bombardment of radiation that resulted in an increase in the earth's cloud cover and a dramatic cooling of the earth (The fifth bowl is darkness and cold).

A nearby supernova explosion continues to be one of the theories that scientists have considered to explain some of the mass extinction's that the dinosaurs and other species have suffered during various ages of the earth's history.

A supernova remnant in the constellation Vela is believed to have exploded 11,400 years ago. The remnant there is 800 light years away in our own galaxy. It was probably as bright as a 7-day-old moon, a magnitude of -10.

The Alpha and the Omega

The birth of the star Arcturus may go back to the very formation of the universe, or at least to the formation of our galaxy. It may soon herald the end of history, as we have known it.

"I am the Alpha and the Omega, the First and the Last, the Beginning and the End." Revelation 22:13.

Christ describes Himself as the First and the Last, exactly as Jehovah does in Isaiah 44:6: **"I am the First and I am the Last, besides Me there is no God."**

The oldest light that can be seen in the heavens with the naked eye may be the same star that brings down the curtain on the nations of the world. Arcturus, the alpha star of the night sky could prove to be the omega star as well.

The last sign

An Arcturus supernova could be the final announcement that Christ's arrival is imminent. Jesus tells us that just before He comes again, the sign of the Son of Man will be seen in the heavens. It is interesting to note that Matthew 24 says when the sign of the Son of Man is seen in the sky all the tribes of the earth will mourn. This reaction will no doubt be caused by the realization that Christ is coming back to judge the world, but seeing a supernova's shock wave speeding toward our planet may be an additional reason for unbelievers to be worried.

A supernova and the resulting cosmic disasters would be both the sign of His imminent return and the means by which the wrath of God is poured out on the kingdom of the Beast. The Brilliant Morning Star has arrived. To those who have received Him, He is their long awaited Savior. To those who have rejected Him, He comes as Judge and put an end to the reign of evil. He comes to crush the Serpent's head.

Arcturus is:

The golden star
The shepherd star
The grape harvest star
The brilliant morning star
The alpha and the omega star
The star that shines from the east
The star that crushes the Serpent's head
The star of the Coming One constellation
The star that walks among the seven lamp stands
The star that holds the seven stars in its right hand

Chapter 5

Comet Wormwood

Satan and his demons are cast out

The dramatic passage in Revelation 12 begins with: **"a great portent appeared in heaven . . . "** This condensed synopsis of the world's future since the time of Christ is set among the stars of heaven. It describes Israel as a woman who is robed in the sun with the moon under her feet and a crown of 12 stars on her head. She gives birth to the Messiah as the Dragon waits to devour the child. Both the woman and her son are snatched away, out of reach of the Dragon. War then develops in heaven between Satan and the archangel Michael. Satan is cast down to earth, but,

"Woe to the earth and sea because the Devil has come down to you with raging anger, well aware that he has but a short season." Revelation 12:12.

The falling star of the false messiah

The seven trumpets of Revelation 8-11 give the details of Satan's fall to earth:

"A huge star blazing like a torch fell from the sky . . . the star's name is Wormwood." Revelation 8:10,11.

"I saw a star that had fallen on the earth from heaven to whom was given the key to the pit of the abyss. He opened

the pit of the abyss . . ." Revelation 9:1.

The Scriptures make only three distinctions between lights in the heavens: the sun, the moon, and the stars. Today our language and knowledge have grown to encompass many names for the objects we see in the night sky: planets, comets, asteroids, meteorites, nebulas, galaxies, etc. But even today we still use some descriptive words that we know are not technically accurate. We say falling stars when we know that they are not really stars but small meteorites or bits of comet dust that burn up as they fall through the earth's atmosphere. What astronomer doesn't use the words "sunrise" and "sunset," when we know that the sun does not actually set or rise but just comes into view and goes out of view as the earth rotates? The apostles and prophets who wrote the scriptures used the limited vocabulary of their time to describe how the unfamiliar phenomena in their revelations appeared to them.

It is obvious that the "star" Wormwood that John is describing is probably a comet. It is the visible manifestation of Satan's fall to earth after his battle in heaven with Michael and the angels. This is the false messianic coming, a terrible and violent event that will be the worst ecological disaster in history up to that time. This falling star will throw a great cloud of smoke and debris into the atmosphere that will darken the sun, darken the moon, and blot out stars. The reverberating impact will cause earthquakes and tsunamis around the world.

"...bewilderment at the roaring of the sea and waves, men swooning from dread and apprehension about events that are about to take place in the world; for the powers of the heavens will be shaken." Luke 21:26.

When a large object from space strikes the earth at such a tremendous speed, it creates a massive shock wave that travels through the planet and comes out the other side, creating worldwide earthquakes and volcanic activity. There is an impact area on the planet Mercury that was actually created by a comet or asteroid colliding with the opposite side of it, sending a shock wave through that planet and fracturing the rock in the other side into huge concentric circles; creating a jumble of shocked geological features there.

The name Wormwood indicates a poisonous substance. This is descriptive of both the physical and spiritual realities of Wormwood and all it represents. It will poison a third of the rivers on the planet. We can get a clue to its impact site from this. It will have to strike a spot where about a third of the planet's rivers flow. The mountainous regions of central Asia might be the best fit.

We have a precedent for a poisonous visitor to our planet: the Tunguska explosion over Siberia early in the early 20th century. An object of unknown makeup exploded and vaporized over a remote site in Siberia without apparently touching the ground. Instantly felling millions of trees, it carried some unknown substance that induced plant mutations. Spectral analysis of comets has revealed poisonous chemicals, such as cyanogen (precursor if cyanide), present in large quantities.

The broken comet

Wormwood will likely fall to earth in fragments, like Shoemaker-Levy. The whole world watched in wonder as this hundreds of thousands of miles long string of a fragmented comet struck Jupiter, making holes in that planet's atmosphere as big as the size of the earth. We can take this event as a forewarning of what is prophesied to happen to our own world. Even if Wormwood is a fraction of the mass of Shoemaker-Levy, it will easily live up to the catastrophic destruction described in Revelation 8.

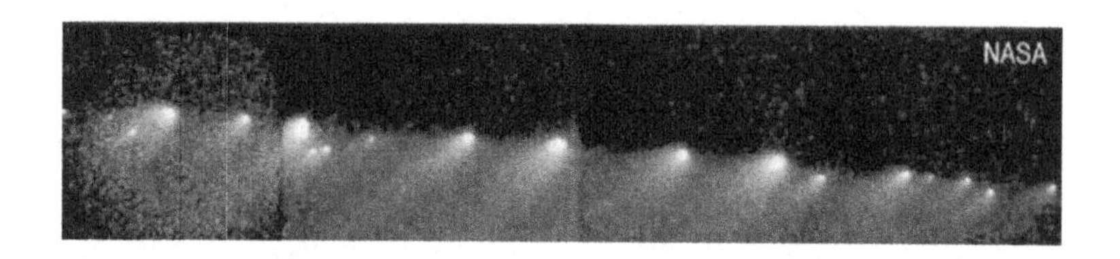

Comet Shoemaker-Levy 9 broken up by Jupiter's gravity in 1993. NASA

Observations have long shown that comets breaking up as they are tugged at by the Solar System's gravitational fields are fairly common. Since most comets have the density of a packed snowball, it does not take much to break them apart. When a comet passes near the Sun in its elongated orbit, the increased radiation heats up its center, weakening it. The strong gravitational fields of the larger solar system bodies like the Sun and Jupiter put tremendous strain on these objects as they race by. These rocky snowballs break apart and the pieces sometimes take different trajectories, or like Shoemaker-Levy, separate into a long string of mini comets hundreds of thousands of miles long.

According to John's description in the Apocalypse, there will be two main pieces of the comet. The first piece will fall into the sea, and the main piece, Wormwood, will fall on land. Both will be preceded by a blizzard of smaller meteorites that will shower the planet. When a comet is approaching the Sun, its tail flows away from the solar wind. As it circles around the back and travels away from the Sun, the solar wind pushes its tail in front of its direction of movement, so that it is actually moving in the opposite direction that it appears to be. If Wormwood has rounded the sun, has broken up, and is on a collision course with the earth, its tail of gas and small debris will likely strike the Earth first, creating an intense meteor storm well before the main body slams into the planet, possibly days before. The stars will certainly appear to fall from the heavens. This vast shower of burning comet debris could cause grass and forest fires all over the world as the earth rotates in this stream.

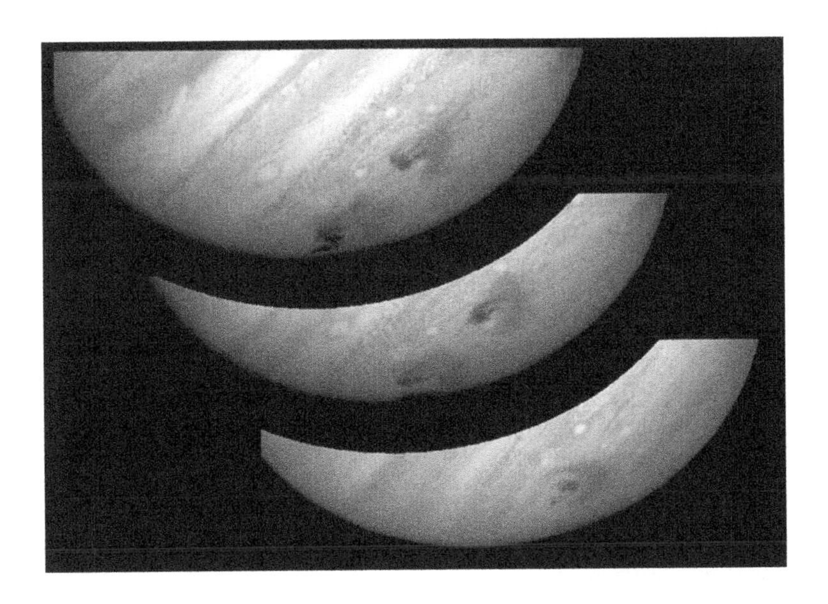

The Shoemaker-Levy 9 sequence of impacts on Jupiter, each about the size of the Earth. NASA

The meteor showers we see at particular times of the year, like the Persieds in the August and the Leonids in November are thin streams of meteor dust and tiny pebbles left by some passing comet. When the earth collides with them at its tremendous orbital speed, the sparse cloud of meteorites flash into brilliant "falling stars" as they burn up in the atmosphere. We call them showers, but on average a meteor streaks across the sky only once every minute or so. Only on rare occasions do meteors fall at hundreds a minute to appear as a shower of falling stars. We could expect the full impact of Wormwood's fragmented tail to create a true shower of meteors, like a hailstorm. People, wildlife, and livestock caught outside during this shower would risk injury or death from this blizzard of burning meteorites. Rocks would hit the earth with the velocities of bullets, causing serious wounds to anyone or anything unfortunate enough to be caught out of doors. Fire mixed with blood.

We can see previews of this rain of fire as we watch news stories that give us an occasional glimpse at the damage small meteors can cause when they strike the earth. One woman was hospitalized when a meteor crashed through the roof of her house as she was sitting on her couch. In another incident, an automobile's trunk was smashed when it was struck by a football-sized meteor.

The stars will fall from the heavens

We can deduce from the first six trumpet blasts much of this entire event:

1st: Hail of fire mixed with blood. One third of the grass and trees are burned up.
2nd: Fiery mountain hurled into the sea. One third of the sea is turned to blood, one third of the sea creatures are killed, and one third of the ships are destroyed.
3rd: Wormwood falls, a huge star, blazing like a torch. It turns one third of the rivers and springs bitter. Many people die of the bitter water.
4th: A blight falls on one third of the sun, moon, and stars. They are darkened for one third of a day and night.
5th: The star (Satan) opens the abyss. The smoke rising from the abyss darkens the sun and the air. Locusts come out of the pit and torture all without the seal of God for five months.
6th: The Four "angels" at the Euphrates and their 200 million strong cavalry kill one-third of mankind.

The "stars" fall from the heavens over the Rocky Mountains during the Leonid meteor shower of 2001. A composite of multiple exposures taken over an hour

Numbers are clues

Certain numbers in the Scriptures are indicative of the source and meaning of certain events. Four is the number of the Creation, meaning it refers to the Creation or originates as a force of nature. One-third is the portion Satan is allowed to destroy, meaning that one-third destructions come directly from the hand of Satan. Six is the number of imperfection, falling short, or of man. Seven is the number of perfection, completion, of God's plan and personal being. Twelve is the number of human regeneration. Three and a half indicates death. A second three and a half added to that is seven, the number of resurrection and eternal life. With this in mind we can describe this cosmic disaster.

It will start with a rain of comet debris. With showers of comet fragments the **"stars will fall from the sky."** These falling stars are the visible counterparts of the demons who are thrown out of heaven along with Satan. A mountain-sized chunk will then fall into the sea, possibly the Pacific Ocean, killing a third of the sea life, turning the sea red, and creating massive tsunamis. Tsunami, a Japanese word, is a great wave of water, hundreds of miles long that breaks over coastlines as it reaches heights of hundreds of feet, bringing sudden, catastrophic destruction to anything in its path. Then Wormwood will fall, bitter, poisonous, and deadly. A great shadow of evil will spread over the planet.

"Woe to the earth and sea, for the devil has come down to you with raging anger, well aware that he has but a short season." Revelation 12:12.

An enraged Satan will be determined to use this short season to destroy as much of the work of God that he can:

"The thief comes to steal, and kill, and destroy . . . "John 10:10.

The armies of the east will be possessed to go on a killing spree of unimaginable viciousness. A third of the world's population, more than one and a half billion people will die in the slaughter (the same number will have already perished in World War III).

"So the four angels . . . were set free to kill a third of mankind. The number of their cavalry was two hundred million." Revelation 9:16,17. (remember four is the number of the Creation. These angels are connected with natural phenomena, perhaps a vast Asian army trying to escape Wormwood's destruction).

50,000-year-old Barringer Meteor Crater in Arizona.
USGS photo by D Roddy

Impact theories

There is a growing interest and concern about comet and meteor impacts on the Earth. Books, web pages, television, and movies describe not just the possibility, but also the probability of another body in the solar system colliding with our planet. In some scientific circles there is alarm that we are not doing enough to prepare for such an event. Many have concluded that the age of the dinosaurs came to an end because of a catastrophic collision with a large meteor or comet. Anyone visiting Arizona can actually peer into a mile wide meteor crater blasted out of the desert rock thousands of years ago. Other impact craters dot our planet; most are disguised by the relentless erosion that eventually erases all traces of these earthshaking collisions. The moon is a silent witness to many of the space objects that have struck it over the eons. Anyone can look into a telescope and see the craters left by meteors and comets that have impacted the moon over the billions of years of its existence.

The red star

John wrote his account of a star's fall to earth almost 2,000 years ago, long before such phenomena were formally studied or understood by any scholars. The detailed descriptions in Revelation and the Gospels are remarkably accurate pictures of what we now know will result from such an event. They also fill in some missing pieces that scientists are just discovering, like the poisonous nature of these comets, the atmospheric dissemination of smoke and debris, as well as the earthquakes and tsunamis that will occur all over the planet. We know that massive amounts of smoke thrown high into the atmosphere could darken the moon to a blood red color, like a lunar eclipse. The sea turning to blood may be a new revelation to scientists who study the effects that a comet may have when it plunges into the ocean. The ice of some comets is described as having a rusty or rosy color. Wormwood may have an even brighter red color than most other comets. The slaughter of sea life on such a vast scale may also contribute to a red sea. The interaction of unknown chemicals from a comet with seawater might be another way to produce a sea of blood.

Moving China

If a fragmented comet were to hit central Asia, cause massive fires, and poison the region's fresh water supply, the great populations there might be forced to migrate to find another source of food and drinkable water. This could be the initial impetus for the 200 million-man cavalry to begin its march westward, killing and pillaging as it goes. The demonic invitation by the Antichrist to join him for his war against Israel and their Messiah would bring them into the Middle East and eventually into the valley of Meddigo for the last great battle of the age, Armageddon:

"...three unclean spirits like frogs . . . They go out to the kings of the whole earth to muster them for the war of the

Sovereign God's great Day." Revelation 16:13,14.

Strange creatures

Cyanide and cyanogen are present in most comets. If these chemicals were released into our atmosphere in the right quantities, the results to humanity might be remarkably similar to the plaques of locusts of the fifth trumpet. Cyanide is an extremely potent toxin. A tiny speck of it on the tongue is enough to kill a person. There would not have to be a lot disseminated into the atmosphere to cause terrible problems. Earlier in the 20th century many believed that the earth would pass through the tail of Halley's comet. There was widespread panic when scientists revealed that cyanogen was present in comets. "Comet pills" were sold by hucksters to supposedly ward off the poisonous gases, but the tail of Halley's comet was much too thin to shower the Earth with any measurable chemical.

"Out of the smoke locusts went forth on the earth . . . power was granted them, not to kill but for five months to torture . . . " Revelation 9:3,5.

The locusts emerge from the smoke of the Abyss that the star Wormwood opens. They sting like scorpions to torture for five months everyone who does not have the seal of God on their foreheads (the seal of God is given to the 144,000 sealed Jews out of every tribe of Israel).

When cyanogen is heated (as in an impact with the earth) it emits cyanide gas. Cyanide gas in small concentrations causes extreme irritation to the eyes and skin. Imagine living in a world where the whole planet's atmosphere is poisoned with a small percentage of this gas. Not enough to kill, but to cause intense irritation. There would be nowhere to escape the stinging torture. Revelation 9:6 says:

"...people will seek death without finding it; they will be anxious to die but death evades them."

If cyanide gas poisons the planet from a comet, it will be one of the great ironies of history. Hydrogen cyanide was the deadly component of Zyklon B that was used in the Nazi gas chambers to murder the Jews and others in the concentration camps. The Zyklon B granules were poured into vents atop the gas chambers where they were turned into cyanide gas by the body heat of the victims inside. God never forgets. His justice is poetic as well as perfect.

John gives a detailed description of the stinging locusts that have no natural counterpart. He tells us that they have as king over them the angel of the abyss, Apoyllon, It is possible that these creatures are not visible but spiritual beings, ugly demons who do their king's bidding by helping to spread poison over the planet. Other possibilities are that they are genetically engineered insects specifically made for war or some genetic experiment that has gone terribly wrong.

The stinging scenario of Wormwood:

A comet plunges into the earth excavating a great pit where a column of smoke rises miles into the atmosphere and spreads out over the earth. The heated cyanogen turns into cyanide gas as it mixed with this vast, hot plume of rising smoke, pulverized rock, and comet material. It then spreads over the globe, darkening the skies and causing worldwide affliction. The world's population takes refuge indoors as billions experience the stinging torture of the poisoned air that is all around them. It takes five months for the cyanogen to be washed out of the atmosphere.

The history of comets

A major comet is seen in our sky about once a decade

or so. A major comet is one that is large enough, with enough ejecting gas and material to be seen clearly and spectacularly in the night sky. Astronomers observe many smaller comets, invisible to the naked eye, almost daily. In fact there is probably a small comet streaking through the solar system right now that is being tracked by astronomers. If you have a good telescope and know exactly where to look you could probably observe one.

Major comets have always generated great fascination and fear among societies throughout history. Ancient astronomers often recorded their appearance and soothsayers attached prophetic meaning to them as either good or bad omens. Our generation has had the privilege to witness one of the most spectacular comets ever seen in history. Comet Hale-Bopp, the comet of the century. This beautiful, classic comet spread across our night sky in 1997 and gave the world a good long look at one of these inspiring cosmic events. As beautiful as they are though, they can be sobering as well when it is considered that our world will some day encounter one of these speeding mountains of rock and ice, perhaps within our lifetime.

The sky will tell the story

The story of history has a beginning, middle, and an ending. The Creator in His sovereignty will use the heavens we see outside our door every night to tell the story of the great events that will precede Christ's return. The Brilliant Morning Star is in preparation to shine over our planet.

The fact that two unprecedented cosmic disasters may occur within the short time of the last days will prove that history, as we know it is coming to an end. An impact by a comet or meteor on the earth could possibly be viewed as just a random event, but a comet impact and a nearby supernova both occurring within a few years of each other could only mean that the ancient prophesies of God's Word are certainly taking place. When these events happen it will be obvious to all that a day of judgment is at hand, but for many it will be too late.

"...everyone, slave and free hid themselves in the caves and in the mountain rocks, and called to the mountains and to the rocks, 'Fall on us and hide us from the presence of the One who is seated on the throne and from the Lamb; for the great day of Their wrath has come and who is able to stand?" Revelation 6:15-17.

There will be no repentance for those who carry the mark of the Beast, only the certainty of judgment and the prospect of an eternity without hope.

"Whoever worships the beast and his statue and receives the mark on his forehead or on his hand, shall drink of the wine of God's wrath that has been mixed undiluted in the cup of His anger, and he shall be tortured with fire and brimstone in the presence of the holy angels and of the Lamb. " Revelation 14: 9,10.

Watch the heavens

Previews have occurred for us to witness if we are perceptive enough to recognize them: comet Shoemaker-Levy, Hale-Bopp, the Tanguska explosion, supernova in distant galaxies, and even the falling stars we see when we look up on a summer night and gaze out into God's vast universe. Ready or not, we may be the generation to see the fulfillment of all that has been written as the powers of the heavens are shaken.

We may receive more previews in the coming years. We can take them as a warning that the earth is not immune from sudden, catastrophic events in our galactic neighborhood.

Comet of the century. Hale-Bopp, 1997. Photo by Wei-Hao Wang

The apparent changelessness of the sky night after night can lull us into a false sense of security. The Word of God has already warned us that history, as we know it, will end in a violent shaking of not only the earth but the heavens as well. Those things that we usually rely upon and take comfort in will not always be there for us, but Christ promises that He will never fail us if we trust in Him alone.

"Heaven and earth will pass away but My words will never pass away." Matthew 24:35.

Chapter 6

Timelines

The end of the world is hard to imagine, especially for those who doubt the truth given to us in the Word of God. Christ and the Apostles tell us that the last days of history will come as an unexpected surprise for the vast majority of people in the world.

"First of all you should understand that in the last days scoffers will come on the scene with their scoffing, behaving in accord with their own lusts, and saying, 'What about His promised coming? For ever since the forefathers fell asleep, everything has remained as it was from the beginning of creation.'" II Peter 3:3,4.

"As were the days of Noah so will the coming of the Son of Man be; for as in those days before the flood people ate and drank, married and were given in marriage until the day when Noah entered the ark, and did not understand until the deluge come and swept them all away, so will the coming of the Son of Man be." Matthew 24:37,38.

Tribulation timeline

To get an idea of how these cosmic events will fit into the period of the last days, we can go again to Matthew 24 to get a general timeline. Christ gives us an overall outline within a few paragraphs of what will happen and in what order. This timeline is repeated in both Mark and Luke. These chapters can serve as a master key to unlock the order of events in the other books of prophecy like Revelation and Daniel.

"You will be hearing of wars and rumors of wars; see that you are not troubled; for they have to come, but that is not yet the end. For nation will rise against nation and kingdom against kingdom, and there will be famines and earthquakes in various places; all these are but the early pains of childbirth. Then they will hand you over to be persecuted...many then will fall away and will betray one another..." Matthew 24: 3-10.

"When you, therefore, see the desolating abomination mentioned by the Prophet Daniel, set up in the holy place - let the reader take note of this - then those in Judea should flee to the mountains...for there will be such great tribulation as has never been experienced from the world's beginning until now, no ever will be." Matthew 24: 15,16,20.

"Right after the tribulation of those days the sun will be darkened and the moon will not shed her light; the stars will fall from the sky and the forces of heaven will be shaken. Then will the sign of the Son of Man be shown in the sky, and all the tribes of the earth will mourn. And they will see the Son of Man coming on the clouds of heaven with great power and glory. And He will send out His angels with a loud trumpet call, and they will gather His chosen from the four winds, from one end of heaven to the other." Matthew 24:29-31.

The Tribulation will start with wars and end with Christ's coming to gather His chosen from the four winds. We can identify seven major events in the order that they occur:

1. The early pains of childbirth - conquest, war, famines, and earthquakes
2. The persecution and apostasy of professing Christians.
3. The abomination of desolation (the Antichrist seats himself in the temple and declares himself god)
4. The forces of heaven will be shaken - the sun and moon will be darkened and the stars will fall from the heavens.
5. The sign of the Son of Man will be seen in the sky
6. Christ visibly comes on the clouds with great power and glory
7. The chosen are gathered from the four winds at the trumpet call

The Revelation timeline

The Apocalypse of John follows these prophecies of the Gospels but adds many details to them. The prophecies of John's Revelation are fairly straightforward if we remember that several parentheses take place between the list of events and some of the seals and trumpets overlap. The timeline would proceed like this.

I. Sudden birth pains - The Four Horsemen:

Seal 1 - Conquest
Seal 2 - War
Seal 3 - Famine
Seal 4 - Death - 1/4 of world (1.5 billion people)
Seal 5 - Persecution of the church

COMET WORMWOOD IMPACTS THE EARTH

Seal 6 - Earthquakes, sun and moon darken, stars fall
(There is an overlap at the sixth seal with the seventh seal's six trumpets, all describing the same events)
Seal 6 = 1st through 7th trumpets

II. The Seventh Seal:

1st Trumpet. Hail of fire mixed with blood
2nd Trumpet. Fiery mountain hurled into the sea
3rd Trumpet. Huge star, **Wormwood** falls on rivers and springs
4th Trumpet. Blight on the sun, moon, and stars, 1/3 is darkened
5th Trumpet. Satan opens the abyss; locusts torture mankind for five months
6th Trumpet. Four angel's 200 million-man cavalry kills 1/3 of mankind (another 1.5 billion people)

III. The Seventh Trumpet - Christ returns and gathers His saints (the resurrection and rapture of the Church).

ARCTURUS SUPERNOVA - SIGN OF THE SON OF MAN

IV. The Golden Bowls of God's wrath:

1. Malignant ulcers plague those wearing the mark of the Beast
2. Sea turns to blood. Every sea creature dies
3. Rivers and springs turn to blood
4. Sun permitted to scorch humanity with terrible heat
5. Beast's kingdom is plunged into painful darkness
6. Euphrates dries up so the kings of the east can invade
7. Worldwide earthquake, superstorms, cities of the nations fall

All of these Tribulation events listed in Revelation are broken by other parenthetical descriptions in John's Apocalypse, giving coincidental details of the last days, they are:

The sealing of the 144,000 Jews
The battle in heaven with Michael and Satan's fall to earth
The rise of the world dictatorship of the Antichrist
The entrance of the tribulation saints into heaven
The destruction of the New Roman Empire
The return of Christ as the conquering King
The invasion at Armageddon and Judgment of the Nations
The seizure of the Dragon, Beast, and Prophet
The millennium, the reign of Christ on Earth
The last battle on earth
The Great White Throne Judgment
The destruction of the universe
The creation of a new heaven and earth
The entrance of the saved into the Heavenly Jerusalem

The Tribulation chart

The following chart details how the Tribulation and Second Coming might be formally illustrated. The seven seals of Revelation cover the entire Tribulation period up to the Day of the Lord, Christ's return. The General Tribulation could be divided into two parts: the Four Horsemen and the Great Tribulation. The keystone of this time line is the Abomination of Desolation, which occurs in the middle of the General Tribulation. Christ's Second Coming may actually be two events: the Mount of Olives return for the Church, and the final coming at Mt Sinai where Jesus descends with His heavenly armies to rescue Israel and destroy the armies of the world.

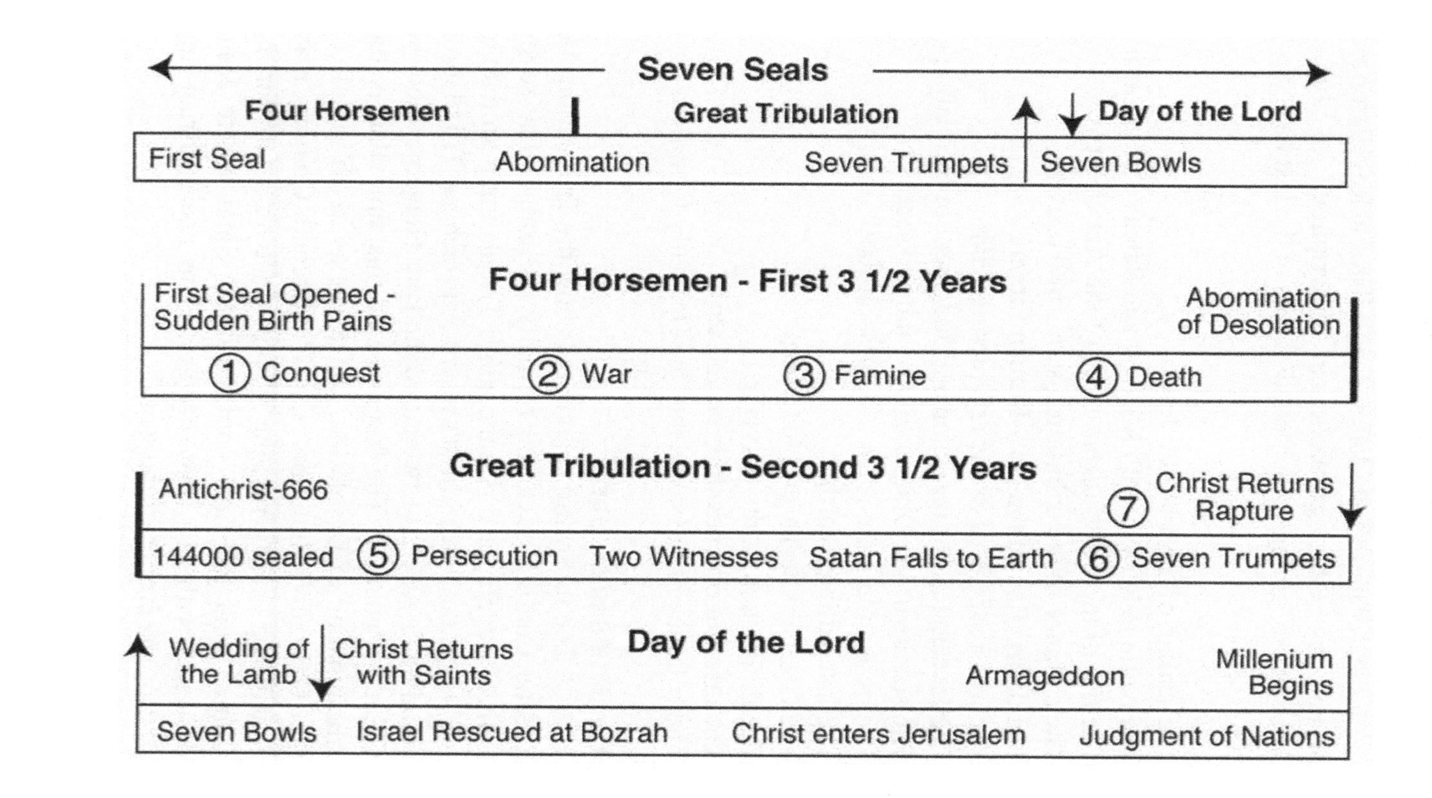

Seven Seals
Four Horsemen
Great Tribulation
Day of the Lord
First Seal
Abomination
Seven Trumpets
Seven Bowls
Four Horsemen - First 3 1/2 Years
First Seal Opened - Sudden Birth Pains
Abomination of Desolation
1 Conquest
2 War
3 Famine
4 Death
Great Tribulation - Second 3 1/2 Years
Antichrist-666
7 Christ Returns Rapture
144000 sealed
5 Persecution
Two Witnesses
Satan Falls to Earth
6 Seven Trumpets
Day of the Lord
Wedding of the Lamb
Christ Returns with Saints
Armageddon
Millenium Begins
Seven Bowls
Israel Rescued at Bozrah
Christ enters Jerusalem
Judgment of Nations

Daniel's seventy weeks

The book of Daniel can also help us put these events into a specific time frame. The well-known seventy weeks of Daniel describes the time Israel has left to prepare for the coming of the Messianic Kingdom. Sixty-nine weeks have already passed, ending with Christ's first coming. The seventieth week has yet to occur and is delayed by the great "parenthesis" of the church age of which we are still in. The last week of Daniel's seventy weeks consists of a week of years. This seven-year period is divided into two parts of three and a half years each, with the Abomination of Desolation occurring in the middle of the seven years. This is the event where the world dictator seats himself in the Jerusalem Temple and declares himself god. As mentioned before, the first three and one half years represents a period that ends in darkness and death and the second three and one half years represents a period ending in light and resurrection, adding up to 7, the number that signifies the perfection of God's completed plan.

The first 3 ½ years are a set up to the second 3 ½ years. The first half ripens the world for the kingdom of Satan, instituted with the Abomination of Desolation when The Beast will rule the world and trample down Jerusalem for 3 ½ years.

Chapter 7

A History of Heavenly Signs

Heavenly Signs in the Scripture

It would be a mistake to believe that every unusual cosmic phenomenon has some spiritual significance or precedes some important event. The Scriptures do not give any weight to this idea. Most spectacular or unusual appearances in the heavens such as comets and supernova have no more meaning than any other natural event. It is only when they are predicted by the Word of God that they truly become a heavenly sign and a spiritually significant event.

The Scriptures also warn against astrology, which is exposed as a false belief mentioned in the same category as necroromancing (talking to the dead) and witchcraft (making magic and casting spells). There is not a single event in the Scriptures that is connected to astrology. The constellations may have prophetic and spiritual meaning as do some other cosmic bodies, but tracking every movement of heavenly bodies to predict the future is both futile and destructive.

"...let the astrologers, the stargazers, and the monthly prognosticators stand up and save you from what shall come upon you. Take note! They shall all be like stubble and the fire shall consume them." Isaiah 47:13,14.

Old testament heavenly signs

Joshua includes the most striking comic sign of the Old Testament. The sun and moon stood still and refused to set.

"Now Joshua spoke to the Lord on the day that He delivered up the Amorites to the Israelites; and he said before the eyes of Israel, 'O sun, wait in Gibeon! Wait in the valley of Ajalon, O moon!' The sun waited and the moon stood still, while a nation took vengeance on its enemies. Is it not written in the book of Jashar, 'The sun stood still in the midst of the sky and did not hasten to set for a whole day?' " Joshua 10:12-14.

A similar phenomenon took place as a sign to King Hezekiah that the proclamation of his imminent death was rescinded.

"And this shall be a sign to you from the Lord that the Lord will do this thing which He has promised: Behold, I will turn back the shadow ten degrees on the dial of Ahaz, on which the sun has gone down. And the sun returned ten of the degrees it had gone down." Isaiah 38: 7,8.

How these signs physically happened has to be a matter of conjecture. Whether the rotation of the earth was actually stopped or some sort of atmospheric lens distorted the sun's true position, or some other event was responsible can only be guessed at. A miracle can be a result either of God's direct intervention in the physical universe or as a result of the perfect foreknowledge of God, predicting the seemingly random events of the natural universe as they coincide with human history.

New Testament heavenly signs

Precedence for a brilliant, unusual star, announcing

Christ's imminent appearance was forever established at His first coming. The Magi call it "His star."

"Where is the newborn king of the Jews? For we saw His star in the east and we have come to worship Him." ...After listening to the king they traveled on and, lo the star they had seen in the east preceded them until it came and rested above the place where the Child was. And on observing the star their joy was boundless." Matthew 2:2,10.

Paul's heavenly sign

Christ appeared to the Apostle Paul with a brilliant heavenly light. Even Paul's companions saw this light, demonstrating that it was probably a physical phenomenon and not a vision.

"But as I was nearing Damascus on my journey, suddenly at noonday an intense light from heaven shone around me, and as I fell to the ground, I heard a voice saying to me, 'Saul, Saul, why do you persecute Me?' ...Now my companions saw the light, but they did not hear the voice of the One who spoke to me . . . However, because of the brilliance of that intense light, I was blinded..." Acts 22:6-11.

This light obviously greatly outshone the sun. Could that blinding light have been some kind of nova or gamma ray burst outside of our solar system?

The false Star of the Morning - the Antichrist

In Isaiah the king of Babylon is called Lucifer (Day Star), son of the morning:

"How you have fallen from heaven, O Lucifer, son of the morning! ...For you have said in your heart, 'I will ascend to heaven; I will exalt my throne above the stars of God .

. . I will be like the Most High!' Yet you shall be brought down to Sheol, down to the lowest depths of the Pit." Isaiah 14:12-15.

This passage is believed by many to have a deeper meaning that refers to Satan himself, but it could also describe the final Antichrist. The Beast will mimic the legitimate star of the morning. He will present himself as the morning star, an attempt to replace God. The comet Wormwood may be predicted by the false prophet and proclaimed as a sign that the Beast is the morning star, the messiah. Wormwood may actually be a returning comet like Halley's that has appeared before in history, so the time of its return might even be predictable.

Jesus Christ, the true Star of the Morning

The Apostle Peter describes who the genuine star of the morning is: Jesus. His dawning light has a personal significance for each of us.

"So we have the prophetic message reaffirmed, to which you do well to pay attention as you would to a light that shines in a dark place until the day dawns and the Daystar arises in your hearts." II Peter 1:19.

The heavenly signs of Revelation

Much of the book of Revelation is set in the heavens.

"A great portent then appeared in heaven: a woman robed with the sun, with the moon under her feet and a crown of twelve stars on her head, was pregnant, and as she agonized in the pangs of her delivery, she cried out. Then another portent appeared in heaven. There was a gigantic; fiery red dragon with seven heads and ten horns, and on his heads seven diadems. His tail swept away a third of the stars of heaven and hurled them to the

ground." Revelation 12: 1-4.

Various personalities make their appearances among the heavens throughout the Apocalypse, such as this one who makes the most dramatic appearance of any angel ever.

"Then I saw another mighty angel descend from heaven, robed in a cloud, with a rainbow over his head. His face was like the sun; his legs resembled fiery pillars, and he had an opened little scroll in his hand. His right foot he placed on the sea, and his left foot he placed on the land, while with a loud voice like the roar of a lion he gave a shout. And as he shouted the seven thunders raised their voices. " Revelation 10:1.

John is told to seal up what the seven thunders speak without writing it, making it one of the great mysteries of Revelation. The Apostle Paul tells us that at the shout of the archangel the dead in Christ will rise and the rapture will begin. The seven thunders probably has something to do with the resurrection and rapture, perhaps identifying the very day. This mighty angel says,

"There shall be no further delay, but in the days of the seventh angel's trumpet blast...the mystery of God will reach completion." Revelation 10:7.

The appearance of this mighty angel and the voice of the seven thunders are the announcement that Christ has returned and His identity as the Son of God and the only Savior is displayed to the world once and for all. No one will ever again have any doubt about whom Jesus is, and who His people are. The mystery of God will have reached completion.

Chapter 8

When Satan Falls to Earth

The glare of the Sun in this NASA photo appears like an approaching comet about to strike the planet

The fall of the comet Wormwood is directly connected to the conflict between Satan and the Church as it evangelizes in the face of vicious persecution by the Antichrist and His world government/religion. When Christ sent the seventy disciples out to evangelize Israel, He remarked on their return, **"I saw Satan fall to earth like lighting."** Preaching the Gospel has a devastating effect on Satan's stature in the spiritual realm.

We see from the Scriptures that Satan has access to the highest heaven where God is enthroned. He must come there to get permission to test and persecute the saints. In the book of Job, Satan comes before God and asks Him to allow him destroy Job's family and fortune in an effort to tempt Job to curse God. In the Gospel of Luke, Jesus tells Peter that Satan has asked permission to sift the disciples like wheat.

This access to heaven that Satan has had for ages comes to an abrupt end when the Devil and his demons are cast out after being defeated by the archangel Michael and his angels. This final war in heaven is a result of the faithful preaching of the Gospel by Christians during the Tribulation in the face of vicious persecution. Revelation 12 says:

"Then war developed in heaven, Michael and his angels battling against the dragon, and the dragon and his demons waging war, but they were defeated; there was no longer any place for them in heaven. And the great dragon, the serpent of old, called the Devil and Satan, the deceiver of all humanity, was forced out and hurled to the earth, and his angels were flung out along with him.

Then I heard a strong voice proclaiming in heaven, 'Now have come salvation, and the power, and the kingdom of our God, and the authority of His Christ, for the accuser of our brothers, who kept accusing them day and night in the presence of our God, has been thrown out. And they have conquered him by means of the blood of the Lamb and by the word of their testimony; they have not loved their lives, even to the point of death. Be joyful, therefore, you heavens, and those who dwell in them. Woe to the earth and the sea, because the devil has come down

to you with raging anger, well aware that he has but a short season.'" Revelation12:10-12.

It is a day of rejoicing in heaven when Satan is no longer allowed to enter there to challenge God and accuse the saints. For the first time in the history of the universe, Satan will become a permanent resident of the planet, losing his place in the third heaven. He is not only here but he is in a rage. Like any enraged, wicked person he will go on a rampage of destruction. Those who have allowed him to control their lives by opposing the message of Christ will be possessed to do things that will shock even themselves. The destruction and massive killing that follow will defy all reason. A third of humanity, one and a half billion people will be slaughtered, added to the one and a half billion that will have already died during the third world war. Isaiah's prophesy that man will become scarcer than gold will be no exaggeration. The population of the world will be decimated by Satan's violent rage and the cosmic plagues of the last days.

Demonic possession will become commonplace as the spirits that are cast out of heaven, as well as those who are released from the Abyss, roam the world looking for willing bodies to occupy. When Jesus cast the legion of demons out of the demonic in Luke's gospel, they begged Him not to send them into the Abyss. The Abyss is evidently a kind of spiritual prison where those spirits, human and demonic who have committed certain crimes are kept in confinement and punishment for the judgment day. They will be released along with the king of the Abyss, Apollyon, who will possess the body of the Antichrist when Wormwood (Satan) falls to earth and is given the key to the Abyss. Satan will become incarnate through the Beast.

During the Tribulation the church is tested and purified, reaching a point of complete trust in and love for

Christ, willingly giving their lives to testify to Christ. Seeing the prophetic events unfolding right before their eyes will give believers a boldness and zeal that they have not had since the time of the Apostles. Certain knowledge that Christ's return is imminent will be a great motivation to endure the persecutions of the Antichrist's world government and faithfully serve the Lord, **"even to the point of death."**

Your deliverance is near

It is common to focus only on the violent events of the Apocalypse, but there are two sides to the story of the last days. The wrath and judgment one of them, but the glory, love, and grace of God is the other. The last days are not just to punish those who reject Christ but also to rescue, reward, and procure justice for those who love Him and have suffered for Him. Christ encourages us:

"But when you see these things begin to occur, straighten up and lift up your heads, because your deliverance is near." Luke 21:28.

Justice and mercy are equally present in the Apocalypse. It is a time to look forward to the earthly reign of Jesus as well as the justice of God. When Christ returns at the seventh trumpet, the 24 elders are heard to say:

"We give Thee thanks, Lord God Almighty, who is and who was, because Thou hast assumed Thy great power and hast begun to reign. The nations raged and Thy wrath has been realized; also the time for the judging of the dead and for the rewarding of Thy bond servants, the prophets and the saints - in fact, all those who revere Thy name, both small and great; also for the destruction of those who are destroying the earth." Revelation 11:17,18.

Sudden birth pains

The Tribulation will begin with a global breakdown in the present world order. The sovereign hand of God is all that keeps the world from plunging into homicidal chaos and brutal oppression. The Scriptures say that in the end times,**"the love of many will grow cold."** As the Lamb opens the first of the seven seals, God will allow Satan to have full reign in the hearts of those who oppose Christ. Sadly, much of the opposition to the Gospel and support for the Beast will come from "Christian" circles. Even today there is a vicious intolerance in the ecumenical movement for Christians who hold up Christ as the one and only Savior. Portrayed as bigots and hate mongers, Bible believing Christians are constantly under attack from political, educational, and religious factions for not conforming to the worldly philosophies of a society that is increasingly hostile to the Gospel. Christ will be rejected even among many professing Christians in favor for a more palatable, popular belief system in the name of unifying all religions. "Diversity" will include every faith and inclination with the exception of course an exclusive faith in Christ. The great apostasy, or falling away of nominal Christians that Jesus predicted will begin. Hundreds of millions will suddenly be ashamed to say they believe in Him alone. Christianity is the world's largest religion. That will change dramatically during the first years of the tribulation as professing Christians come under immense pressure to abandon their faith.

Opening the seals

The first seal is opened and one of the four living beings shouts "Come!"

"Then I looked and saw a white horse, and its rider holding a bow. To him a crown was given, and he went out conquering and to conquer." Revelation 6:2.

The identity of this horse and rider that kicks off the Tribulation has fueled a lot of speculative theories, but Christ begins his prophesy on the last days with a warning to His disciples not to be deceived by people claiming to be the Christ. This rider on the white horse is a false Christ, most likely the Antichrist himself, promising world peace. He begins his efforts to conquer the world, not by arms, but by crafty political manipulation. He is given a crown, which may indicate that he is voted into the leadership of some body like the United Nations or the European Union. Although purporting to bring world peace, he will be responsible for starting World War III, similar to the Second World War except the death toll will be in the billions instead of millions. By today's population figures, one and a half billion people will die in this war and the resulting destruction of the manufacturing and agricultural infrastructures of the world.

Famine and disease will follow in the footsteps of the slaughter of World War III. In Revelation 6 a voice says,**"a quart of wheat for a day's wage..."** The average wage of a person in a western country is about $150 dollars a day. If you calculate what a bushel of wheat would cost from this, you can conclude that a single farm truck full of about 200 bushels of wheat would be worth about a million dollars.

Life will become cheap as people engage in a desperate, selfish fight to stay alive. The true nature of unbelievers and Christians alike will be revealed, as Christ says,

"...the hour of trial that is coming upon the whole world, to put to the test those who live on the earth." Revelation 3:10.

The Tribulation will be like a curtain that is pulled aside to once and for all reveal the true nature of every belief system of mankind, Christian and nonbeliever alike; graphically showing who the world is really following, God or Satan. The events of the last days will erase all illusions of religious neutrality. As the Antichrist gains control of the world's economic and political powers, the pressures to submit to His mark will be nearly inescapable. No one will be able to say they do not belong to the Beast with his mark on their forehead or hand for all to see.

Days of the beasts

Revelation tells us that even wild animals will partake of the slaughter. Today predators are making a comeback in many parts of the world as they are being protected by the ecology movement. Many species have also adapted to an urban world, finding ways to thrive in city and suburban environments. Bears, wolves, coyotes, cougars, and other predators will take a toll on the starving hoards of refugees searching the country sides for food. Even the earth's creatures will conspire against humanity to bring God's judgment down on the nations.

The fifth seal will bring about the events of the sixth and seventh seals. The fifth seal reveals the saints under the altar in heaven who have been martyred during the Tribulation. They call for justice but are told to rest a little longer until the number of their brothers who are to be killed as they have been is completed. The war in heaven between Satan and Michael is an intensified conclusion of the battle that occurs every day in the spiritual realm as God's people go out into a hostile world with the good news of Christ. The last 7 years of history will be a time of super righteousness played against a background of super evil that will heat up the heavenly conflict to the eventual outcome that Satan and his demons are soundly defeated and kicked out for good, but:

"Woe to the earth and sea, because the Devil has come down to you with raging anger, well aware that he has but a short season." Revelation 12:12.

What follows will shake the Earth to its foundations: the impact of comet Wormwood.

Asteroids, earthquakes, volcanoes

Even though both Wormwood and Arcturus will produce earthquakes, there are other causes of earthquakes during the first years of the last days. These precede both the comet impact and supernova. These are tied to the world conflicts that begin the birth pains of the Tribulation, a physical manifestation of the spiritual turmoil shaking the globe. As mentioned before, the spiritual and physical universes are connected. Great events in the spiritual realm can cause corresponding events in the other. Some say that earthquakes have been increasing in the last century but the physical cause of this is not clear. If the geological structures of planet Earth have been going through some unusual changes lately, most people seem to be unaware of the fact. This phenomenon may be much more apparent after Christ opens the first of the seven seals, beginning the countdown of the seven years of the Tribulation. People living in earthquake prone areas should take note of this.

An asteroid impact is another possibility of fulfilling some of the destruction of Revelation 8 and 9. It is possible that both a comet and an asteroid impact could happen within a short time, although an asteroid alone would not cause the variety of plagues that we see in these chapters. As unlikely as it would seem, a comet could collide with a near-earth asteroid and send both of them plunging into the planet. The second trumpet, an immense mountain blazing with fire that is hurled into the sea, could be an asteroid, as well as a large chunk of the fragmented comet Wormwood as mentioned before.

An asteroid impact is statistically more likely event. Our planet is dotted with craters from them. NASA and other groups routinely track near-earth asteroids in case one gets too close for comfort. Recently, a small asteroid has actually passed inside the orbit of the Moon. There are so many swarming around our solar system that only a fraction of them have been identified and tracked. Most are too small to cause anything but local destruction, about the size of a car or house, but a medium, block-sized asteroid's impact would be felt around the world. A city-sized asteroid would cause world wide destruction, maybe even the extinction of the human race.

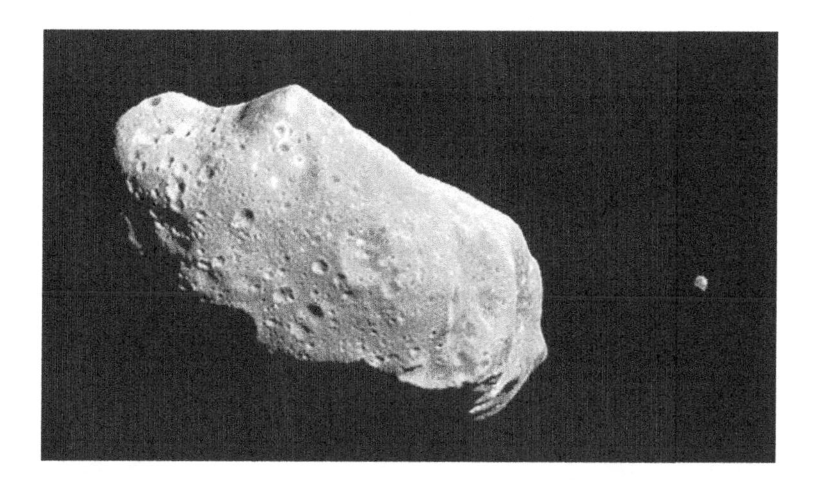

The asteroid Ida with its own moon, Dactyl. Ida is 35 miles long, one of the largest asteroids. An asteroid this size would cause worldwide destruction but it doesn't come near the Earth's orbit. NASA

Most asteroids travel at a slower velocity relative to the earth than comets do. Also, the average comet is much larger than the average asteroid. The combined impact energy and thus destructive power of a comet would be greater if it hit us than if an asteroid impacted. Still, an asteroid could add its destruction to the terrible plagues of the Last Days.

Major volcanic eruptions fit many of the plagues of the Last Days mentioned in prophetic Scripture. Mt St Helens. USGS photo by Austin Post

Volcanoes are another ingredient that will likely cause destruction in various parts of the globe. The worldwide earthquake tremors resulting from a comet striking the earth, as well as the shockwave of a nearby supernova, will no doubt shake up a certain amount of volcanic energy, especially in those areas where volcanoes are already active. New volcanoes may also be born in areas where there were none previously. The Scriptures describe rains of fire and brimstone (sulfur) as another ingredient that adds to the plagues of the Last Days.

Chapter 9

The False Messiah

Most of the major prophetic Scriptures have a lot to say about the Antichrist, the individual who rises out of the turmoil of World War III to become a world leader. He will rule when both Wormwood and Arcturus impact the Earth. His kingdom may be strengthened by Wormwood but ravaged by Arcturus. His crowning achievement will be his conquest of Israel and seating himself in the Temple as god. This is the day that Satanic evil will finally dominate the entire planet and proceed in its attempt annihilate all opposition. Christians will be hunted down and killed for their faith in vast numbers. Revelation tells us that the Beast will be allowed to conquer the saints, bringing an effective end to the preaching of the Gospel throughout the world. It will be a difficult but hopeful time, as many Christians will still survive to await the Coming One.

The Antichrist may use the chaos of the comet disaster as a strategy to gather the world's armies into the Middle East to annihilate the remaining Jews who will gather to await their Messiah.

There is an tremendous amount of detail in both Revelation and Daniel about the Beast. A long list of attributes of this last evil dictator can be gleaned from the Scriptures:

1. Antireligious - blasphemes God

2. Makes a god of himself
3. Has no love for women
4. Boastful, proud, arrogant
5. Extremely clever and skilled in political manipulation
6. Worships military strength
7. Power not from arms but from political intrigue
8. Many false signs and miracles
9. Possessed by a 1st century spirit who arises from the Abyss
10. Wars against and conquers the saints
11. Authority over every people, language, and nation
12. Suffers a head wound and appears to rise from the dead
13. Is an eighth king; six reigned before or during Roman times
14. Is one of three kings that "breaks off" the other two
15. Is given worldwide power by 10 temporary kingdoms
16. Will help destroy the Great Harlot, the New Roman Empire
17. Will gather the world's armies at Armageddon
18. Sets up a statue to himself to be worshiped by all
19. His mark, representing his name and 666, will be forced on all who participate in the world economy.
20. Works in conjunction with a prominent religious figure to force the world to worship himself and eventually, Satan.

The Antichrist will kick off the Tribulation by entering the social and political arenas in the name of a one world government. He will proceed to strengthen his influence by helping to destroy the current balance of power and plunging the world into war. He will then be handed leadership of a confederacy of 10 nation, establishing himself as the single most powerful world leader. By 3 ½ years into the Tribulation he will have succeeded in taking over Israel, stopping Jewish worship and declaring himself the messiah and god. He will wage a vicious, murderous war on Christians and Jews who refuse his mark and will manage to put an end to the spreading of the Gospel and the practice of Judaism. By the time the Tribulation comes to an end, most people left in the world will wear his mark and worship his statue; by then only about a third of the world's population will still be alive. A remnant of Jews - 144,000 (12,000 out of each tribe of Israel) will be kept safe from his murderous reach in the "wilderness" for the second 3 ½ years of the Tribulation. They will be immune to the plagues and persecutions under the special protection of the seal of God.

The return of Barabbas?

One of the amazing facts about the Antichrist is that he will, at some point, be possessed by the spirit of a 1st century personality. This is the one, **"who was and is not and is coming ... the beast that comes up from the abyss..."** Revelation 11:7. John says that the Antichrist was in the world during his writing of John's first epistle but had apparently died by the time John wrote Revelation 11:7. John says in his letter that he was in the world, but by the time Revelations was written he, **"is not."**

One of the Roman Emperors is most often mentioned as this spirit who waits in the Abyss to posses the body of the Antichrist. Another likely candidate could be Barabbas, the murderer who was released by Pilate in place of Christ. There is no record of what ever happened to Barabbas. True to Scriptural principals, his existence is open ended (Melchizedek is described as having an eternal office because the Scripture records no beginning or end to his appearance, just as the prophet Elijah's mantle is still open because he never died).

Barabbas means "son of the father," which could only mean son of Satan. This may be a reference to the unholy trinity of the Dragon, the Beast, and his prophet; father, son and satanic spirit. The number 666 also refers to this trinity, one six for each member of it.

Barabbas was most likely a bandit/revolutionary; probably hated for his robberies and murders but admired for harassing the Romans, a sort of 1st century Poncho Villa. Because he was chosen to be released by the Jews who opposed Jesus, they might have inadvertently made him a major figure in the great spiritual conflict that will come to a head during the final period. There are some scholars that think that Barabbas' first name was also Jesus (which is the Greek form of Joshua) and that Pilate was really saying, "Which Jesus shall I release for you, Barabbas or the Christ?" (Matthew 27:17). Jesus was a common first name among 1st century Jews, as it is among Hispanics today.

The name of the Antichrist may be Joshua or Jesus Barabbas, or some similar equivalent in another language, like "savior, son of the father," or "anointed one, son of the father." Within this name three persons are mentioned, illustrating the unholy trinity of 666.

The false Resurrection

The demonic-like possession of this world figure who becomes the Antichrist will likely occur when he receives the head wound and comes back to life. Modern medicine can bring people back from a state of brain death, many experiencing an out-of- body journey into the realm of the dead. This near death may give the Beast an opportunity to possess the body of this world political figure. Satan himself also possessed Judas Iscariot at the last supper to fulfill his role in betraying Christ.

This false resurrection will be a major reason why so much of the world's population will follow and worship the Beast. The promise of eternal life without repentance or faith in God will be an irresistible attraction to a world that wants to live forever but doesn't want to repent and follow the true Savior.

The Beast's ideology will shift from atheism, to

worship of himself as god, and eventually to open Satan worship under the priesthood of the Beast's prophet.

There is much speculation about who the Antichrist will be, with various contemporary world figures routinely identified by prophecy students as being the Beast.

The Proto-Antichrist

Daniel gives a prophetic description of a historical figure as the prototype of the Antichrist: the evil Antiochus IV, the Greek king who inherited control over Israel from an ancestor of one of Alexander the Great's four generals. Antiochus tried to destroy the Jewish religion, going so far as defiling the Temple in Jerusalem by butchering a pig there.

Seleucid King Antiochus IV who calls himself Epiphanes, or "god incarnate" on the reverse of this coin. Courtesy of David Kaplin, "Coins from Famous People in History." http://members.aol.com/dkaplan888/main.html

Zechariah prophesied a final conflict between the son of Zion and the son of Greece at the Second Coming.

" I will incite your son O Zion, against your son, O Greece, and I will make you as the sword of a mighty man. Then the Lord shall appear above them, and His arrow

shall go out as lightning; the Lord God shall give a blast on the ram's horn, and He shall move in the tempest of the south." Zechariah 9:13,14.

Like the proto-Antichrist, the final Antichrist will be of Greek lineage, possibly from one of the countries north of Israel that made up ancient Greece: present day Greece or Turkey, or possibly Syria, Lebanon, or the Balkans.

Daniel describes the Antichrist as the king of the north who will battle with a king of the south, with Israel in the middle. In the coming world war, the Middle East will become a battleground between two empires, north and south of Israel. He will succeed in taking over the state of Israel, not by force, but by crafty political maneuvering, then gaining control over their remaining nuclear weapons. He may disguise himself as an ally as Israel is in danger of being overrun by the Islamic countries. He may also gain their trust and allegiance by helping to build their Temple in Jerusalem.

The United States may have been neutralized either militarily, politically, or both. An expensive, ruinous war in the Middle East or Asia might throw America's political and economic systems into chaos. The cultural conflict between liberal humanism and Judeo-Christian beliefs could even degenerate into a civil war. A radical socialist government could come to power in the US, destroying personal freedom and religious liberty, abandoning Israel and washing its hands of further involvement in the Middle East. Israel may no longer be able to look to America for military or financial support. The Beast will then show his true nature and take over Israel as dictator, stopping all Christian and Judaic worship, and seating himself in the Temple.

Under the burden of uncontrollable warfare and destruction, the ten empires of the new world order will turn over their remaining militaries and nuclear weapons to this false messiah in the hope that a worldwide, centralized government will finally bring peace. The Beast will be a master of deception, a man with a golden tongue, who will be able to convince world leaders to trust him.

Mark of the Beast

There are three labels for the Beast: the name of the Beast, the number of the Beast, and the mark of the Beast. Of these three we are clearly given only one, the number, which is the well-known 666. This number refers to the satanic trinity: the Dragon, the Beast, and the Prophet, one six for each. Six is the number of imperfection or falling short of God's perfect number, seven. This mark will have to be worn on the forehead or right hand and will be a symbol for three sixes. The graphic symbol for the number six is the pentagram. Three pentagrams should prove be the mark of the Beast .

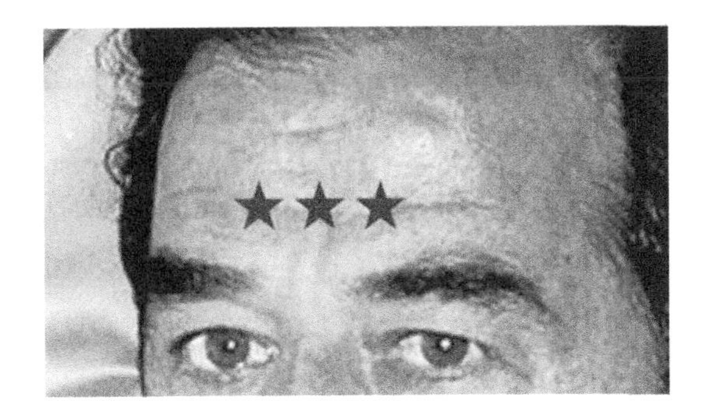

Tattooed with the Mark of the Beast

The pentagram is an ancient symbol used in religion and the occult. It is also a graphic representation of man, with a head, two arms and two legs illustrated in its five points. The heart or torso of the pentagram is the sixth part. Revelation tells us that the number of the Beast **"is a man's number."** The pentagram by itself is simply a symbol for man. How this symbol is used determines if it takes on a sinister meaning or not. In witchcraft the pentangle is used with the "head" of the star pointed down, illustrating man worshiping Satan. When it has a circle around it, it represents the exclusion of God. When it is repeated three times, it takes the form of a trinity, replacing God with an unholy trio.

The tripentagram mark

Three pentagrams may become trendy in pop culture, tattoos, and as religious and political symbols in the coming years, especially in the one-world movement. Currency may begin to show up with three pentagrams. Also look for a world figure who uses it as the symbol of his movement the way Hitler used the swastika. There are institutions and governments that have already adopted this design, unaware of what it may really signify. The pentagram is the most widely used graphic on national flags.

The pentangle illustrates the six parts of the pentagram

There is a lot that has been said about a microchip implanted under the skin as being the mark of the Beast. This may well be used but by definition a mark appears on the skin, not under it. The mark will likely be just a simple tattoo or brand, easily made by anyone, anywhere in the world. Some may try to hide it and wear it only on their right hand, but many will doubtless wear it proudly on their forehead. All credit cards, bank checks, and currency will have to carry the tripentagram mark to be accepted in the world economy. During the Tribulation no one will be allowed to buy or sell without wearing this permanent mark.

A tripentagram in the stars?

Finally, notice that head of the constellation Serpens Caput, the serpent's head, is made up of a triangle of three bright stars. The Mark of the Beast may also be instituted as a triangle of stars:

This could be the ultimate mark of the Beast

The false prophet

The Prophet is described as second beast who arises from the land, while the Antichrist arises from the Sea. These descriptions are symbolic of where these personalities come from. The Sea represents the world, the Gentile nations. The land represents the Promised Land, Israel; so the Antichrist will be a Gentile and his prophet will most likely be Jewish, from Israel. This false prophet may claim to be Elijah and proclaim the Antichrist as the messiah. His false miracles will fool many into following. Many professing Christians will also be deceived into accepting his message. He will likely precede the appearance of the Beast on the world stage, being a popular religious or occultic leader, to prophesy the coming of this false christ.

The current teachings of Judaism, which insists that the Messiah has not yet come, will serve to deliver the Jews and Israel right into the hands of the Antichrist. This Jewish religious leader will use false signs to convince them that he is Elijah the prophet and the Antichrist is the messiah who will unite all religions and bring peace to the world. This Jewish "prophet" may even be considered the messiah himself by some, just as John the Baptist was rumored to be for a time.

The Antichrist's fake resurrection from the dead will then secure worldwide belief in his divine origins. He may also make a false claim to the line of David in order to ingratiate himself to the Jews.

Chapter 10

Israel and the Temple

Jerusalem - Dome of the Rock and the Mount of Olives from the Citadel

The events that surround the Temple in Jerusalem will be one of the keys to beginning the seven year countdown to Christ's Coming, probably the most important indication that the Tribulation is beginning or about to begin. It is clear that the Jews have to reestablish Temple worship of some kind to begin the 70th week mentioned in Daniel. It will be an extremely difficult task to accomplish and might come be at a cost of much blood and suffering; perhaps even a major war in the Middle East.

Israel in the last days

The Jews and Israel play a central role in the Tribulation. It is the last week of years given them in Daniel to prepare for the coming of the Messiah's Kingdom by sanctifying themselves and the Temple's Holy of Holies. The Old Testament prophets deal primarily with the Jews and Israel, just as the New Testament writers focus on the Church. As John the Baptist said about Jesus when He came the first time, **"He must increase, but I must decrease."** The mission of the Gentile Church will decrease during the Tribulation and Israel's will increase. The Tribulation is really the time of the Jews again in God's plan as the time of the Gentiles comes to an end. The age of the Church is completed as the exact number of Gentile believers predestined long ago in the plan of God is reached:

"...I want you not to be ignorant of this secret: partial insensibility has come over Israel until the full number of Gentiles come in..." Romans 11:25,26.

This is reflected in the scroll that John is given that is sweet in his mouth, but bitter to his stomach, that is, the church's experience will be first sweet, then bitter during the Tribulation. An uncountable host of Gentile believers will enter the Tribulation as an influential force in the world before being mercilessly conquered by the Beast, bringing an effective end to the age of the Church.

In the Old Testament the prophet Ezekiel is also given a scroll, but it is at first bitter, then sweet. This foretells Israel's experience during the Tribulation as their nation and worship are taken from them but are powerfully restored when Christ returns to establish His Kingdom in Israel. A remnant of Israel will then take center stage amid the troubles of the last days as the surviving Jews complete their return to Israel from all over the globe and resist the tyranny of the Beast and his mark, but as Jeremiah said of Jacob's troubles, **"...he will be saved out of it."** Christ will return to rapture the Church and confront the Antichrist as the Beast's armies invade Israel and surround the beleaguered nation.

Wailing Wall on the west side of the Temple Mount

The Jews will have their Temple and worship during the Tribulation for three and a half years. Establishment of the state of Israel came after the Holocaust of twelve million European Jews. The reestablishment of worship in the Temple in Jerusalem could also come at a high price, most likely after a war against surrounding Arab states. The Muslims will never allow their third holiest shrine, the El

Aqua Mosque and Dome of the Rock, to be destroyed and replaced with a Jewish Temple without an all-out war against Israel. The Israelis have always been well aware of this fact, this is why they have let the Muslims control the Temple Mount and have humiliated themselves at the wailing wall, a scrap of the wall along the west side of Herod's 1st century temple complex.

The Antichrist may play a key role in rebuilding the Temple. The fact is, Satan wants the Temple rebuilt as much as anyone else because Jerusalem is where he intends to ascend the throne of God. Through the Beast, he will set up his throne up in the Temple and demand to be worshiped by all the world.

The act of destroying the Moslem buildings on the Mount Moriah and rebuilding the Temple there could be the impetus for starting World War III and mark the beginning of the Tribulation. The Beast will be the one who starts it all if he is the driving force that replaces the Moslem building with a Jewish Temple.

A major war in the Middle East appears to be a certainty soon, especially with the increasing radicalization of many Islamic religious sects. Israel and the Jews are the ultimate targets of these belligerent, murderous forms of Islam. The Israel-hating instigators of these movements are leading their people into the destruction of their own nations by putting themselves under the judgment of God. The Arab countries would be ruined by a major war which would make them easy prey for outside conquest by one of the imperial powers that will rise out of the new world order during the Tribulation. Their oil will make them an attractive prize.

70 weeks left for Israel to prepare

The seventy weeks of Daniel's prophesy is a deadline for the Jewish people as a nation to sanctify themselves and the Temple before Messiah returns to set up His Kingdom on earth. Sixty-nine weeks of years have already taken place. The countdown was stopped at the first coming of Christ.

In Daniel's description of the 70 weeks, the last week is set aside by itself. This is the last seven years that God is going to grant Israel to prepare itself for the second coming of the Messiah. The intervening age of the Church is really an age of grace to give the Gentiles and individual Jews an opportunity to receive Messiah the Lamb, and be saved before Messiah the King returns to claim His throne and judge the nations. The Holy of Holies must be consecrated within these 70 weeks as well. Why? One answer could be that something has to be placed there: the Ark of the Covenant?

Chapter 11

The Ark of the Covenant

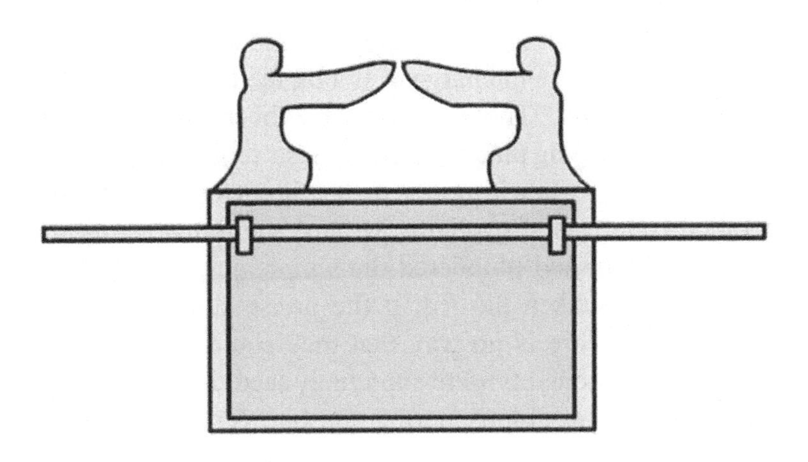

The Ark of the Covenant was the most sacred artifact of the Temple. The very presence of God rested there. The Scriptures mysteriously omit everything about its disappearance.

One of the ways the events of the last days might be set in motion is by the recovery of the Ark of the Covenant. It is certainly still in existence because we see it in heaven in Revelation 11:19. The last mention of the Ark in the Old

Testament is in Jeremiah when he says that it will not be missed or made again during the Messiah's millennial reign. King Josiah, a contemporary of Isaiah, ordered the Levites to put the Ark back into the Temple in about 620 BC. This is the last time the location of the Ark is mentioned in the Old Testament.

It is evident from the historical books of the Old Testament that the Ark was moved in and out of the temple by the priests, depending on the political climate of the times and the risks from invaders. When David fled Jerusalem after his son Absalom usurped his throne, the priests tried to follow him with the Ark but he ordered them to take it back to the city. It was a very portable relic and it is evident that the Levitical priests in charge of it took their duty to protect it very seriously. There might have been underground passages and hiding places that the priests took advantage of whenever an apostate king was on the throne or an army had invaded Israel. The Egyptians, Syrians, and Babylonians all took Jerusalem and plundered the temple and would most certainly have taken the Ark if the priests did not hide it somewhere. There is no way that they could ever let this happen, as its contents were supremely sacred. Even priests that took part in idolatry during apostate periods probably would still have had enough sense left to protect the Ark. Of course the sovereignty of God has to always be acknowledged. All the armies in heaven and on earth could not destroy the Ark if He decided that it was going to be safely kept somewhere. And no one is going to find it if it still exists on earth until He is ready to have it recovered.

During the Babylonian siege of Jerusalem, King Zedekiah managed to escape at night between the walls of his garden and get as far as the plains of Jericho before being overtaken by the Chaldeans. Many ancient walled cities had secret tunnels leading out of them for strategic purposes. It is not hard to believe that the priests could have spirited the Ark away at night even under the noses of the Babylonians laying siege to Jerusalem.

Jerusalem is riddled by tunnels, many that have been found and certainly some that have not. The Ark might be hidden in one of these tunnels or in a cave somewhere outside the city. It was not placed in the second temple when the Jews returned from the Babylonian captivity to rebuild the Temple. It was not placed in Herod's Temple. Considering the importance of this object, it most certainly would have been taken to a very secure hiding place. It may be near one of the cities that the Levites lived in. These priests would know these areas intimately and have known the best hiding places there. Israel, because of its types of geology, has a lot of natural caves, many that are known, some that are not, still others that have been used as tombs for centuries.

The Dead Sea Scrolls are a good example of how the caves of this country can be lost and forgotten for thousands of years. These oldest known copies of Old Testament books lie hidden for almost two thousand years until they were found by accident in the 1940's.

Archeologists usually uncover cisterns and underground storage vaults when excavating the ancient cities of Israel. One of these dry, forgotten cisterns could also be an excellent hiding place, perhaps underneath an old temple or synagogue or even under a Levite's house somewhere.

But if the Ark were suddenly found, what would happen then? There is a possibility that its discovery would not be made public, given the unstable political climate of the Middle East. Just finding it could set off a war. If it were found in Palestinian territory that might also prove to be a serious problem. It might even be found by one of Israel's enemies. Even though digging up antiquities is a punishable crime, people are caught on a regular basis with metal detectors looking for coins and antiquities. These artifacts find their way to antiquities dealers where they are legally sold to the public. Could one of these relic thieves stumble upon the Ark of the Covenant some day just like the shepherd who found the Dead Sea Scrolls?

Ark of the Covenant found?

There are some who claim to already know where the Ark is or even to have found it, but with no real supporting evidence. Some say it is in another country, Ethiopia or Ireland, but again without a bit of evidence.

An American archeologist claimed to have found not only the Ark but to have photographed it. It was supposed to be in a cave under Gordon's Calvary, an alternate site of the crucifixion. He gives no evidence to corroborate this, either physical or photographic (He also claims to have also found Noah's ark, the true Mt Sinai, and Pharaoh's chariots in the Red Sea). His photographs look intentionally blurry and murky. No ark in these pictures.

Some Jewish Rabbis in Jerusalem claim to have almost found the Ark in a tunnel under the Temple Mount before the authorities stopped them, again without any real evidence.

Another team claims to have seen the Ark in a cave on Mt Nebo in Jordan. No evidence.

If the Ark is really in a cave or tunnel somewhere, other artifacts from the Temple would most likely accompany it, perhaps even earlier copies of Old Testament texts than the Dead Sea Scrolls; possibly even the original texts of some of the books. It might also include the breastplate of the high priest or other worship utensils. A treasure trove might be waiting to be found somewhere in Israel or another country that would make both King Tut's tomb and the Dead Sea Scrolls pale in significance.

The whereabouts of the Ark is usually connected with Jeremiah the prophet because he was God's spokesman during the time of the Babylonian invasion when the Temple was sacked. A Levitical priest, he would be the most likely person to take responsibility for the Ark, especially since the Lord told him well ahead of time that Jerusalem would be captured. Could he have had it taken to his hometown of Anathoth? The book of Jeremiah tells us that he bought a field there during the siege of Jerusalem. Is this field where he could have buried the Ark?

Jeremiah's story ends in Egypt where he was forced to accompany the remaining Jewish rulers against God's commandment never to go back to Egypt. It is possible that the Ark accompanied them to Egypt, although unlikely. In Egypt, Jeremiah writes one of His prophesies on a scroll and places it under the threshold of the Pharaoh's palace. Could he have hidden something else there too? Perhaps directions to the Ark's whereabouts? Is there a clue in Jeremiah's book of prophecy that points to where the Ark is hidden? Is there another book of the Bible that gives such a clue? Could someone else have taken the Ark? There is an Ethiopian legend that the Queen of Sheba's son stole the Ark when visiting Solomon and took it to Ethiopia where it still resides, guarded night and day. This is impossible since the presence of the Ark in Jerusalem is mentioned well after Solomon's time.

The problem with an invader sacking the Temple and stealing the Ark is that when it is moved or touched by anyone but sanctified Levitical priests, it brings death and disease to its captors. The Philistines captured it and suffered a horrible skin disease until it was returned. Non priestly Israelites then peered inside and many died as a result. Even a well-meaning priest tried to steady the Ark as it rode in a tipping cart and died instantly for touching it. It just isn't possible for anyone but the designated priests to be in possession of this physical representation of God's covenant with His people. If it still exists, it must be handled properly only by the right people.

For Christians the ark is part of the Old Covenant and so would not be important for worship. Under the New Covenant, the body of every believer is the temple of the Holy Spirit. For Jews, however, the significance of the Ark's recovery would be incalculable. It would be inconceivable that the recovery of the Ark would not lead to the rebuilding of the Temple in Jerusalem. The Jews have worshiped for two thousand years without a Temple and most seem to be content to continue to do so. They had complete control of the Temple Mount during the 1967 war but immediately turned it back over to the Moslems. They know that to try to take over the Temple Mount to build a temple would lead to an all-out war with every Arab country in the Middle East as well as probably every Islamic country in the world; one that strategically they could not win. If, however, there were a major war in the middle east as an escalation of the present conflict, they would certainly win such a confrontation and this could give them a window of opportunity to go ahead and destroy the Moslem shrines there and build their temple. In any scenario it would most likely take much bloodshed to regain the Temple Mount, rebuild their Temple, and reinstate their worship there. It is also possible that the Israelis might build a Temple in Jerusalem somewhere other than the Temple Mount.

Chapter 12

The Impeder

Paul assures the Thessalonians that the rapture could not have already taken place because the apostasy and the abomination of desolation must happen first. He goes on to explain that an impeder or restrainer was in place at the time that prevented the Antichrist from yet being revealed.

"...he seats himself in the Temple of God with the claim that he himself is God. Do you not recollect how I told you this when I was still with you? So you know now what impedes his being revealed at this time. For the mystery of lawlessness is already at work; only the one who is impeding now will do so until he is taken out of the way. Then will the Lawless one be revealed..." II Thessalonians 2:4-8.

This mysterious impeder has caused a great deal of speculation over the centuries. Various theories have identified it from everything from the Holy Spirit, to Michael the archangel, to the United States of America.

Removal of the United States from the world stage could easily lead to the kind of world war described in the first four seals. The US has served as the world's policeman, keeping various conflicts from escalating. World leaders know that they can go just so far in their aggressive activities, because the US will intervene if their conflicts endangered world peace. The problem with this theory is that there is no indication that Paul was taking about a particular country that would arise 170 centuries later, but of some entity that was active at the time he wrote this.

The archangel, Michael, plays a prominent role in the final period, being mentioned in both Daniel and Revelation. Neither describes him as being taken out of the way, but instead he is fully engaged in the heavenly conflict with the Dragon.

If there were a pretribulation rapture, the Church or the Holy Spirit could be the impeder, but we see from Revelation that Gentile Christians are certainly still on earth in great numbers during the Tribulation. If the Church is here, the Holy Spirit must be present as well.

In spite of the wild speculation, we can assume that the Apostle Paul must have also mentioned this impeding force or personality in his other letters, but likely using different language to describe it.

The Impeder is...

The Impeder is in fact Moses.

"Yes, until now, whenever Moses is being read, a veil lies over their hearts..." II Corinthians 3:15.

This impeder was working when Paul wrote his letters as it is still working today. He gives us a clue when he describes the Antichrist as the lawless one, suggesting that the impeder is the antithesis of this.

The Impeder really has a dual purpose, to keep the Antichrist from being revealed, but also to blind the mind of those who seek righteousness through their works. The Law of Moses, meant to be a vehicle to bring Israel into a close relationship with God, had instead become an end in itself;

religious people preferring to work out their own righteousness instead of accepting His Salvation. Because the religious authorities rejected the gift of His Son, God turned the Law into a stumbling block and a veil to cover their eyes.

"...as it is written, 'God has given them (Israel) **a spirit of stupidity - eyes that do not see and ears that do not hear, to this very day.'"** Romans 11:8.

When the veil of Moses is finally removed, it will mean salvation not only for the Israel as a nation, but victory for the Church as well.

"For if rejection on their (Israel's) **part means the world's reconciliation, what must their acceptance mean but life from the dead?"** Romans 11:15.

On that day there will be no more prerequisites for the age of the Gentiles to end and so the resurrection and rapture of the Church can take place:

"I want you not to be ignorant of this secret: partial insensibly has come over Israel until the full number of Gentiles comes in..." Romans 12:25.

The Beast annihilates Judaism

The proto-Antichrist, Antiochus IV, tried to completely wipe out the Jewish religion in the 2nd century AD, forbidding circumcision, burning all copies of the Law, and making it a capital offense to possess the Scriptures. He crowned his abominations by sacrificing a pig on the altar of the Jerusalem Temple.

Of the end of Judaism, Daniel tells us,

"...in the middle of the week he will cause sacrifices and

offerings to cease. Then on a wing of horrors shall a desolator come to bring ruin until a fully determined end comes down on the desolation." Daniel 9:27.

The latest abomination against the Temple. The sacking and destruction of Jerusalem by the Romans in 70 AD as shown on the arch of Titus in the Forum of Rome

The Beast will take control of Israel and proceed to destroy all observances of the Law, eventually setting himself up in the Temple as god. When the Mosaic Law is wiped out, the Beast will be revealed for what he truly is. His satanic origins may be a shock to the unbelieving Jews, but most believers will certainly be aware of what he is up to.

Paul says the impeder will be taken out of the way. This suggests that he will be forcibly removed. The Impeder is referred to as both something and someone. Moses is the person and the Law is the thing. The Antichrist will use force to obliterate every trace of Judaism and the Mosaic Law from the world. Every Scripture, every menorah, every phylactery, every prayer shawl, every synagogue, every ritual, and every religious practice will be banned, removed, or destroyed when the Beast takes over the world. The power that Antiochus IV had to destroy Judaism is nothing compared to the power that the Antichrist will possess. The Scripture tells us that he will succeed at whatever he undertakes.

The **"wing of horrors"** predicted in Daniel may describe the fall of Satan to earth and the plagues of Wormwood that will wreck havoc with the planet until Christ returns and puts and end to the nightmarish reign of the Beast.

Moses the Impeder

During the Exodus, Moses was not allowed to take Israel into the Promised Land because he struck the rock instead of speaking to it as God commanded. The rock that gushed forth life-giving water to a thirsting Israel symbolized Christ Himself. Moses' act of striking it symbolized Jesus being stricken by the Law at His crucifixion, taking on Himself the penalty of lawlessness and sin for the entire world.

When Christ challenged the Jewish religious leaders, they opposed Him with their purported allegiance to Moses:

"You are his (Jesus) disciple, but we are Moses' disciples. We know that God spoke through Moses; but this fellow - we do not know where he hails from." John 9:28.

"Do not imagine that I shall accuse you before the father; your accuser is Moses, in whom you are hoping. For if you believed Moses you would believe Me, since he wrote about Me." John 5:45,46.

Joshua, the prototype of Christ, was the one chosen to replace Moses and lead Israel across the Jordan River into the Promised Land. Moses, even though a great man of God, embodied the anger of the Law; and so was not allowed to enter. Moses had to be taken out of the way before Israel could cross the Jordan. He had become an impediment then as the Law is now. When it is finally left behind by the Jews, Israel will enter the promised land of the New Birth with the everlasting Joshua: Jesus. Moses and the Law will be forced out of their lives, and without that veil, as well as everything else taken from them; great numbers will finally see that their only hope is in Christ.

But the removal of the impeder will also mean the lawless one will be able to exercise world domination without the opposition of truth from the Scriptures. The Antichrist will attempt to destroy all religion that is based on the Word of God. You can burn all the Torahs, you can destroy all religious objects, you can physically force someone to stop an activity but you cannot destroy what a person truly believes in. Israel will still be free to trust Christ as their Redeemer.

Israel's flight

In the last three and a half years of the Tribulation the Jews who have not received the mark of the Beast will be scattered. Christ tells His followers to flee to the mountains when they see the Abomination of Desolation set up in the Temple. Revelation 12:6 describes Israel's flight into the wilderness from the serpent:

"...the woman fled into the wilderness, where God had a retreat prepared for her to be cared for there during twelve hundred sixty days." (3 ½ years, the second half of the Tribulation).

Revelation 12 provides more details of the Jew's escape into the wilderness:

"The serpent poured water like a river out of his mouth after the woman, that she might be swept away by the stream, but the earth opened its mouth and swallowed the river which the dragon had poured from its mouth. And the dragon, enraged at the woman, went off to wage war against the rest of her offspring, who observe the commands of God and adhere to the testimony of Jesus." Revelation 12 15-17.

Here we see that both Israel and the Church are mentioned together as being present during the second half of the Tribulation. Israel has fled the Dragon into the wilderness, and the Church then bears the full brunt of Satan's rage.

The escape on eagle's wings

"...but to the woman were granted two wings of a giant eagle, so that she might fly to her retreat in the wilderness where, away from the presence of the serpent, she will be cared for during a time, times, and half a time." Revelation 12:14.

This was written 1900 years before the invention of the airplane. These eagles' wings may indicate that Israel's retreat is at a great distance from Israel. You wouldn't fly to Jordan or Syria from Israel. It is also safe to assume that it is not in any populated area. Christ tells them to flee to the mountains. The retreat may be in some remote range such as the Russian Urals or Canadian Rockies, places where it would be possible to hold out for years at a time. Some may go to an even greater distance: Space?

It is important to note that the retreat in the wilderness

will be specially prepared, and the woman is cared for there. It is likely that none other than the Church will prepare this safe haven and care for Israel during her stay in the wilderness.

There will likely be a broad underground movement opposed to the Beast's one-world government/religion. Not just Christians and Jews, but other rebel groups as well. It won't take a genius to figure out what is going on in the world. The Scriptures tell us that the Jewish children will return in the arms of kings and queens. Some world leaders will secretly play a part in helping Israel survive the pogroms of the Antichrist and return them to Israel. There will likely be a great deal of resentment of the Antichrist's pervasive power and some national rulers will help the Jews return to Israel even though they are forced to give outward allegiance to the Beast.

Still, the great destruction caused by the four horsemen will no doubt take its toll on Jews as well as Gentiles. The deadly wars and famines will decimate the world-wide population of Jews just as it will all other ethnic groups. If people become scarcer than gold by the beginning of the Millennium, Jewish populations too may be reduced dramatically. Israel may prove to be the safest place for them, at least until the Antichrist sets up his abomination that causes desolation. Then the time to flee into the mountains will come.

The valley of the Mount of Olives

"His feet shall stand in that day upon the Mount of Olives, which is on the east side of Jerusalem, and the Mount of Olives shall be split in the middle eastward and westward by a very great valley; half the mountain shall move northward and half southward. You shall flee (through) **the valley of My mountain."** Zechariah 14:4,5.

The Mount of Olives will be split by a great valley as Christ sets foot there when He returns

When Christ returns to set foot on the Mount of Olives, it will be split into an east-west valley. The new valley will become a protective highway for the Jew's flight. It will keep Israel safe as the sea of armies of the Antichrist that surround Jerusalem are parted as well. Reminiscent of the parting of the Red Sea, the Messiah will part the earth itself for Israel's escape. Christ will step into the role that Moses and Joshua prototyped to become Israel's ultimate Deliverer.

"I will whistle for them and gather them...I will bring them back from the land of Egypt; from Assyria I will gather them...They shall pass through the sea of trouble..." Zechariah 10:8-11.

The Scriptures describe Bozra in Edom, modern day

southwest Jordan, as a sanctuary for the Jews before their final return to Jerusalem when Christ comes again. The route they take back to Jerusalem from Bozra may well be through the valley of the Mt of Olives.

"I will certainly collect the remnant of Israel; I will collect them like a flock in a fold; like a herd in the midst of its pasture." Micah 2:12.

"Who is this who comes from Edom, with crimson stained apparel from Bozrah, the One adorned in His apparel, marching in the greatness of His might? It is I, the One speaking righteousness, mighty to save! ...I have trodden the wine press alone..." Isaiah 62:1,3.

Bozrah means sheepfold. Bozrah is believed by some to be one and the same as the lost city of Petra. It is at Bozrah where Christ will personally, singularly, slay the armies that are poised to annihilate the remnant of Jews hiding there.

Only a remnant will be saved

Only a third of the Israelis will survive the pogroms of the Beast to be saved at Christ's return.

"...two parts in it shall be cut off, shall perish, and the third shall be left in it. But I will bring the third in with fire; I will refine them as the refining of silver, and I will test them as the testing of gold." Zechariah 13:8,9.

This remaining third, this remnant, will consist of Jews who have been refined in the extreme circumstances of the Tribulation. Their character will be forged into a clear recognition of true faith apart from contrived piety. Their thirst for God will be pure, without any pretenses of legalism or self-righteousness.

"A remnant, the remnant of Jacob, will return to the mighty God. For though your people O Israel, be like the sand of the sea, only a remnant of them will return." Isaiah 10:21-23.

"The sun shall be changed into darkness, and the moon into blood, before the coming of the day of the Lord, dark and terrible; but everyone who calls upon the name of the Lord shall be saved. For in mount Zion and in Jerusalem there shall be those who escape, as the Lord has said." Joel 2:30-32.

"...I will gather all the nations to Jerusalem to wage war. The city shall be captured...half of the city shall go into captivity; but the rest of the people will not be cut off from the city." Zechariah 14:2.

Israel and Armageddon

There appears to be two main groups of Jewish survivors of the Tribulation when Jesus returns: those in Jerusalem and those in the wilderness who will eventually be gathered in Bozrah. The vast armies of the world will surround the Jews of the tribe of Judah. The billions of attacking troops will also spill out of the valley of Meddigo and down into the Great Rift Valley, the Jordan Valley and Dead Sea area. They will surround Jerusalem and Bozrah where the last people of Israel are hiding. Christ will descend with his heavenly armies and will destroy the hoards that surround Israel at Bozrah. Like the first Joshua, He will then lead them from the wilderness across the Jordan. Through the valley of the Mt of Olives, Israel will return to Jerusalem as the sea of armies intent on destroying them is parted as well. Christ will enter Jerusalem through the east gate and begin His reign and judgment of the nations.

The last of the Gentile believers

Undoubtedly, the way Gentile Christians have conducted themselves during the Tribulation will have an immense effect on the Jews who resist the Beast and his number. Christians will face death by the millions rather than submit to Antichrist worship. Evangelicals will likely be the last and only group to support the Jews in their right to possess the land of Israel. They will also play an important role in protecting Jews from the persecution of the One World Government. When the Jews are forced to escape the Beast's tyranny, it will be true believers (not the apostate church) who will protect them, feed them, and help them escape from danger. The protection of Israel will become the major function of the Church once intense, worldwide persecution is under way against both Evangelical Christians and religious Jews.

When the Temple worship is reestablished, the time of the Gentiles will be nearly at an end. There will be nothing left for God to accomplish by the Tribulation except the conversion of Israel. This leads us to the real purpose of the Tribulation; to purify the Church and make it ready to meet Christ and to then bring Israel back to their true Savior; to destroy everything they rely upon so they will realize that Christ is their only hope. The very heavens above them and the earth under their feet will be shaken. Even the Law will be taken from them. There will be nothing left to believe in but the One who gave Himself for them.

A great number of Jewish people will come to faith in Christ during the Tribulation to join the Church as He appears, welcoming Him with open arms.

"You will no longer see me until you say, 'Blessed is He who comes in the name of the Lord.'" Matthew 23:39. These are the Jews of today, who represent only two tribes of Israel, Judah and Benjamin (and Levites). The complete

Israel, all twelve tribes, **"all Israel will be saved,"** will stay on the earth after the rapture to be gathered from around the world as Jesus Christ establishes His Kingdom in Israel.

The lawless one

As the Antichrist gains power over the political, military, and economic institutions of the world, he will initiate a vicious campaign to wipe out all religion. The first thing any tyrant does is to destroy the opposition. Christianity and Judaism will be his primary targets. These faiths provide the world with its only true ethical foundation and opposition to every kind of evil. Even for unbelievers, Biblical guidelines in society provide restraint against immoral excess. As the Scriptures are viciously repressed, lawlessness will win out and the lawless one will be free to do as he wishes, even demanding to be worshiped as god. Most people in the world today think that lawlessness is freedom. They will find out that is not true when the Antichrist rules. The world will feel free to reject truth and virtue, following him to their eternal destruction.

Raw idolatry will dominate the world as the Beast sets up his statue that all must bow down to and his mark that all must wear. There will be idols of the Beast all over the world, people bowing down to them just as in Biblical times. Blatant Satanism will then become the One World Government's official religion. There is always a natural progression from atheism, to personality worship, and finally to occultism as we see in societies that have become officially atheist. Humanity is always compelled to worship someone. There is no such thing as a spiritual vacuum. If God does not fill the human soul, Satan will always oblige.

The final rejection of Christ by the world will ensure most people will be deceived by the flashy "miracles" of the Beast and his prophet.

"The coming of the lawless one is according to Satan's working, with great power and signs and miracles, all of them false, and with limitless deceit of wickedness for those who, because they did not welcome the love of truth for their salvation, are going to destruction. And for this reason God visits them with a delusion that operates on them to believe the falsehood, so that all who have not believed the truth but have taken pleasure in wickedness may be judged." II Thessalonians 2:9-11.

Chapter 13

The 144,000

So now we have three groups of Jewish people that make their appearance in the prophesies of the final period:

1. The surviving half of Jerusalem's Jews
2. The 1/3 remnant saved from the land of Israel
3. The 144,000 Jews with the seal of God on their forehead

These 144,000 are not ordinary people. Even by the standards of the new birth they are extraordinary humans. Imagine someone who has never lied, is celibate, faultless, and follows Christ everywhere. Even the best saints are not this pure.

"These were redeemed from mankind as first fruits for God and for the Lamb." Revelation 14:4.

First fruits of God are always the first born, offered according to the Mosaic Law. These are the first-born sons, who like Samson, Samuel, and John the Baptist are like Nazarites, dedicated by their parents solely to God. They join the Lamb on Mt. Zion, as the judgment of the nations is about to take place.

A nation of newborns

These may in fact be infants and unborn children;

baby boys who will start the Millennium specially dedicated to the King, 12,000 out of each tribe of Israel. They may be filled with the Holy Spirit from birth just as John the Baptist was.

In Jeremiah's great chapters about Israel's return and restoration, chapter 30 and 31, there is not a single mention of any adult Jewish men returning to Israel. Only women and children are specifically mentioned! In fact women and children are described again and again in these chapters:

"Take note, I will bring them from the north country, and gather them from the extreme corners of the earth; among them the blind and the lame, the woman with child and she who is in labor; together, a great company, they shall return here." Jeremiah 31:8.

"...they (Rachel's children) **shall return from the land of the enemy. There is hope for your future, says the Lord; your children shall return to their own country."** Jeremiah 31:17.

Isaiah also predicts a great migration of Jewish children back to Israel:

"I will lift up my hand to the nations; I will raise high My hand to the peoples, and they shall bring your sons in their arms, and your daughters shall be carried on their shoulders. Kings shall be you foster father and their queens your nursing mothers . . . I Myself will save your children." Isaiah 49:22-25.

Imagine a hundred and forty-four thousand or so women some pregnant and some with infants, gathered on Mt Zion in Jerusalem as the armies of the world surround the city. In fact the entire nation of Israel may literally be born on a single day as they are gathered from around the globe.

Isaiah may be speaking of this instant nation of newborns that may be more literal than symbolic:

"Who ever heard of such a thing? Who ever saw its like? Shall a land be brought forth in a single day? Shall a nation be born in a moment? Yet Zion had hardly travailed, when she gave birth to her children . . . Then you shall be nursed, carried upon the hips, and be dandled on the knees. As one whom his mother comforts, so will I comfort you; in Jerusalem you shall be comforted." Isaiah 66: 7,8,12,13.

Incredible migrations

The 144,000 sealed out of each tribe may be the miraculous rebirth of the 10 lost tribes of Israel. How this will actually happen is a mystery, but modern genetics may play a key role.

But where do they come from? The Prophets tells us that Israel will return from the north. In the final period the kingdoms of Israel and Judah will be reunited. When the Assyrians captured the 10 tribes of Israel and took them away, they must have taken them north, but how far north, into Greece or even farther? As slaves they could have been traded from nation to nation, and become so dispersed so as to lose their identity completely over the centuries.

The survivors might have ended up in the remote reaches of what is now Russia, possibly even as far as the Arctic Circle. Imagine a Jewish burial ground in the far north, hidden under the permafrost for thousands of years, their DNA virtually intact.

People in ancient times traveled far more widely that we give them credit for today. China has unearthed incredibly preserved mummies with blond hair and wearing tartan, the plaid fabric of Northern Europe. These European migrants came from thousands of miles to the west and lived for centuries in the deserts of China around the time of the Pharaohs, more than three thousand years ago. The horse cultures of the Asian steppes traveled easily over thousands of miles of grassland and desert, much like the plains Indians of North America who followed the bison herds. These great central Asian plains stretch far north where permafrost can keep buried bodies intact almost indefinitely. The ability of permafrost to keep organic material, including DNA, intact over thousands of years is best illustrated by the way it has preserved ice age mammals like Mammoths that went extinct tens of thousands of years ago.

The soft tissues of the famous Ice Man found in the Italian Alps were well preserved in spite of being frozen since the early Bronze Age, more than four thousand years ago.

Valley of dry bones: symbolic or real?

The graphic story in Ezekiel about the valley of dry bones that the Lord commands Ezekiel to prophesy over,

"You dry bones, hear the word of the Lord . . . I will lay sinews upon you, clothe you with flesh, cover you with skin, put breath in you, and you shall live, and you shall know that I am the Lord." Ezekiel 37:4,5

It is natural to assume that this prophecy is just symbolic. But there may in fact be a specific valley somewhere in the world that contains the bones of the lost tribes of Israel. Modern genetic science may prove to fulfill this prophecy. As scientific research advances, DNA is being extracted from organic material that was considered impossible years ago.

Lost tribes is Greece?

The rise of Greek civilization is one of the most unique events in world history, an unparalleled explosion of art, philosophy, social, and political advances. There may be a deeper spiritual reason for the rise of this civilization. It may in fact coincide with the dispersion of the 10 tribes of Israel into Greece. The Jewish people are a uniquely gifted nation. Even today the artistic and intellectual arenas of western nations have a disproportionately high percentage of Jewish participants. Jewish contributions help create a cutting edge that advances art and science at a phenomenal rate. If this is the case, one thing is certain: modern genetics will prove it. The lost tribes won't be found just on a map, they will be found in a genetics laboratory. Some Greek people may in fact be Jewish unaware, carrying the 10 lost tribes of Israel in their DNA.

Jews deep in Africa

Recently, a group of people in southern Africa, proved to be genetically Jewish, although indistinguishable in appearance from other black Africans. They practiced a vaguely Judaic religion, including circumcision. Scientists traced their DNA to a tribe of Jewish priests by a genetic marker that occurs only in those Jewish men. They were believed to have sailed to Africa from an Arab country where they lived for a time after the Dispersion. Over the centuries they intermarried with Africans so as to lose their Semitic features, but their memory of who they were as well as their unique genetic information has remained intact for thousands of years.

Chapter 14

Sudden Birth Pains

If Arcturus is the sign of the Son of Man, we can use it as a reference point to make a guess at what time of the year the Tribulation will start. Arcturus becomes the morning star in late October until early December. The Tribulation will be about seven years long. The term, "a time, times, and half a time" is three and a half years. There are two three and a half year periods in the Tribulation, divided by the Abomination of Desolation, the Antichrist's takeover of Jerusalem and the Temple. These three and a half year periods are not exact periods of time, but approximate periods. They could be as much as a month longer or shorter than exactly three and a half years.

If the Tribulation is about seven years long, then counting back seven years from an appearance of an Arcturus supernova, and Christ's coming, we can assume that the Tribulation will begin in the fall, sometime in September or October. Yom Kippur and the Jewish feast of booths usually take place around this time. It may be wise to pay attention to world events at this time each year. Some significant event in September or October could signal the beginning of the seven years of the Tribulation.

What will the beginning be like? The first seal is the beginning of conquest by the false Christ. He will initiate his schemes of achieving world power. Then nation will rise against nation, and kingdom against kingdom; World War III will begin. The Scriptures describe it as sudden birth pains. It will all happen with little warning for unbelievers. Then comes the Day of the Lord. The Apostle Paul describes this Day when he writes,

"...they day of the Lord will come as a thief in the night. When they say, "Peace and safety," then sudden destruction will come upon them like the birth pangs of a pregnant woman, and there will be no escape." I Thessalonians 5:2-3.

The prophet Malachi mentions the, **"...great and terrible day of the Lord."**

Zechariah says, **"Behold, a day is coming which is the Lord's . . . for I will gather all the nations to Jerusalem to wage war."**

Joel says, **"The day of the Lord is very great and terrible, who can withstand it?"**

Jeremiah: **"Alas! That day is great; there is none like it. It is a time of distress for Jacob; yet he shall be saved out of it."**

Isaiah: **"Wail for the day of the Lord is at hand... Behold, the day of the Lord comes! For the stars of heaven and its constellations shall not give their light; the sun shall be dark at its rising and the moon shall not send out its light."**

The Day of the Lord is that time when God will put the world to its final test and faithfully fulfill all the promises He has made to His people over the centuries. Specifically, it refers to the appearance of Christ and the wrath of God as it is poured out on a world that worships the Beast. The explosion of Arcturus will bring sudden affliction to those who are proclaiming the "peace and safety" of the Antichrist's kingdom. A deceived world will believe they have finally achieved world peace by crushing Christianity and Judaism and setting up their one-world government.

The 1987 Supernova blasts out into the surrounding stars of the Large Magellanic Cloud. NASA

The seven seals cover the entire seven years of the Tribulation, followed by the Day of the Lord, that time when the Lord returns to passes judgment on the nations. A seal represents a mystery, a revelation that will take place, or is taking place, as the seal is broken.

A trumpet is an announcement that a very important event is about to occur. Wormwood is the announcement that the King of Kings will shortly return. The seven trumpets of the comet Wormwood are the climax of the reign of evil that is the seven years of the Tribulation.

The seven golden bowls represent the direct judgment of God Himself, the pouring out of the wrath of God on the Kingdom of the Beast and the world that follows him.

Sudden birth pains

It is surprising how quickly events in the world can change. In World War I, a single assassination gave the Europeans an excuse to plunge the world into war. In the 1930's Hitler and the Nazis took over Germany and went to war after the war that was to end all wars. In the 40's and 50's one country after another fell to Communism, threatening the very existence of the free world. Today Islamic fanaticism and post-Communist dictatorships threaten world peace and the ideals of democracy, freedom, and God-given human rights.

The terrorist attacks on the US and Israel has again brought the world to the brink of another world conflict; aggravated by the return of the radical forms of socialist politics here and in Europe, there appears to be some classic signs of serious troubles ahead.

China, ever resentful of America's support of Taiwan, has been looking for an opportunity to invade that island for a long time. Their brutal invasion and annexation of Tibet proves their willingness to expand wherever they think they can get away with it.

The Communist parties of North Korea, Laos, Cambodia, and Vietnam have all managed to maintain their tyrannical grip on their oppressed people while threatening the freedom of the countries around them. Castro is still in power in Cuba and in Latin America Communist rebels are spreading terror and fighting to overthrow many of the nations there. Communism is far from dead.

If Christ were to open the first seal shortly, these simmering conflicts would erupt into full-scale wars. The United States may not be able to cope with all of them. Its economic and military resources would soon be exhausted. A full-scale war with China could, as much as it seems inconceivable, mean a military defeat for the US. How are you going to defeat an enemy with a 200 million-man army and nuclear weapons? Given the history of the European countries' slow and insipid responses to world crisis, even on their own continent, they would probably not be much help.

China, with American companies pouring their money and technology into it, has become a superpower very quickly. There is little keeping it from achieving military and economic parity with the US in the near future. There is no doubt that as soon as the Chinese are confident that they can win a war over Taiwan, they will launch an invasion. With the US occupied in the Middle East, that opportunity might be irresistible to them. North Korea would surely also take the opportunity to invade South Korea again.

Russia is still vacillating between democracy and dictatorship. Given their history, another totalitarian state will arise there to again threaten Europe and the Middle East. The vast spiritual vacuum that atheist communism left when it fell has not been filled by an embrace of the Gospel, but instead the occult, anti-Semitism, and gangsterism.

Attitudes also change just as quickly as world events do. Christians and religious Jews will find themselves under increasingly hostile pressure to conform to the social norms of the day in the name of unity and peace. Religious persecution will become common even in western countries. Freedom of speech and religion will be one of the first casualties of a world at war.

A majority in the United States may begin to question if support for Israel is worth the price. When all the nations of the world abandon Israel or become hostile to the Jewish state, you can expect the hand of God to be raised against them. Their days as sovereign nations are numbered.

Israel will undoubtedly feel pressure to make unwise alliances instead of trusting their true Messiah to fight for them. That will be their greatest mistake and will deliver their country into the hands of the world dictator.

Israel has an impressive nuclear arsenal. They could probably repel an invasion to annihilate them. Because of their nuclear capabilities, the Antichrist would have to use diplomacy and deception to subdue Israel, most likely in the guise of an ally and protector.

Return of slavery

The Tribulation will mean the return of true slavery. Millions of conquered people will be bought and sold just as they were in the old Roman Empire. Several Scriptures in Revelation mention slavery in the future:

"...everyone, slaves and free hid themselves in the caves and in the mountain rocks . . . " Revelation 6:15.

"...no longer will anyone buy their cargo of . . . bodies and souls of men (after Babylon's destruction)." Revelation 18:11-13.

Dress rehearsal for the Tribulation

We can learn a little more about the events of the last days by studying the prototypes of them in the Hebrew Scriptures. One of the most complete foreshadowing of these difficult times is in I and II Kings. The story of Ahab, Jezebel, Elijah, and Elisha tell of a time that previews the Tribulation and Second Coming. Even though these characters lived out this drama thousands of years ago, they were also foreordained to give us a glimpse into our future.

Ahab represents apostate Israel, Jezebel is idolatrous

Rome, Elijah represents the Church, and Elisha is believing Israel. The Syrian king, Ben-Hadad plays the role of the Beast. Jehu is the conquering King, the anointed one who brings judgment on Israel's enemies and zealously fulfills the prophecies.

The story starts with the near annihilation of Judaism by the marriage of Ahab and Jezebel and ends in the destruction of Israel's enemies by Jehu, the conquering king. Some of the important details of this story concern the relationship between Elija and Elisha. Elisha becomes a protégé of Elijah. When they cross the Jordan together a chariot of fire separates the two, as Elijah is taken bodily into heaven. Elisha is left to take up Elijah's mantle with a double portion of his spirit.

When the Church is raptured, the Jews will take up the mantle of the Holy Spirit but in an even more miraculous and powerful way than the Church has ever done. As the remaining Jews in the wilderness witnesses the rapture and Second Coming they will finally accept Jesus as their Messiah. This remnant will then return in the power of the Holy Spirit from east of the Jordan to reoccupy Israel. The Antichrist will call the world's armies to assemble in the Valley of Meddigo to attack them. Christ will then reappear on a white horse as the conquering King, bringing justice to Israel and destroying their enemies.

Chapter 15

The Real Rapture

The prevailing belief among Evangelicals is that the rapture will happen before the Tribulation begins. This doctrine is broadly taught as an indisputable fact. The problem with this is that not a single verse of Scripture states that this will happen. A pretribulation rapture was not even considered among Evangelicals before it was proposed in the 19th century and was popularized by a system of theology called Dispensationalism. It was further entrenched among Evangelicals by the Scofield Reference Bible and adopted by most fundamentalist Christian colleges and seminaries.

The vehemence with which the pretribulation rapture is preached and defended with is sometimes shocking, especially since it is one of those doctrines that cannot be directly supported by Scripture. Added to this problem is the fact that many verses of Scripture clearly place the rapture after events of the Tribulation period are well under way.

When the Reformation began it was considered to be just a "squabble among monks," nothing more than a rancorous theological debate, but it eventually split Europe in two and forever changed the basic way Christians believe and worship. The rapture debate could also be considered just doctrinal hair splitting, after all, if you are not still alive when it occurs it doesn't make a great deal of difference whether you believe it will happen before, during, or after the

Tribulation. However, if you are among the generation that is here when the events of the last days begin to unfold, its importance is immense. You do not want to be wrong about this one. Imagine believing that you will be raptured before the Tribulation begins but instead finding yourself among the extreme circumstances of the final period, completely unprepared for it, spiritually or strategically.

The creative interpretations and invention of ideas unsupported by clear statements in the Scriptures that come from teaching a pretribulation rapture is disturbing. The most disturbing is the invention of the secret coming of Christ where believers suddenly disappear without anyone else on the earth realizing what happened. Jesus specifically warned His disciples against expecting a secret coming. Christ's second coming is always described as bodily, visible, and very spectacular; an unprecedented world event that will fill believers with joy as they are caught up to be with Him, and unbelievers with anguish as they realize that they are about to be judged. John tells us,

"Behold He is coming on the clouds and every eye, even those who pierced Him, will see Him, and all the tribes of the earth will beat their breasts over Him." Revelation 1:7.

A pretribulation rapture makes it necessary to start the church all over again since the church is clearly here during the tribulation period, as Revelation 7:9&14 tells us:

"... there was a vast host that no one could count out of all nations and tribes and peoples and tongues . . . These are the ones who have come out of the great Tribulation and they have washed their robes and have made them white in the blood of the Lamb."

This vast, uncountable number of Gentile believers from all over the globe exactly fits the description of the Church as it is today. As missionaries have gone out to every country in the world, millions of people around the world have accepted Jesus as Savior. They will go into and come out of the Tribulation as the Church, tested and purified.

No way around II Thessalonians 2

Apostle Paul in II Thessalonians gives one of the clearest statements supporting a posttribulation rapture. He is assuring the Thessalonian believers the rumors that the second coming and rapture had already occurred were false because certain events have to happen first:

"Now we beg of you brother, with regard to the coming of the Lord Jesus Christ and our meeting together with Him, not to allow your minds to be readily unsettled or disturbed, either by spirit, or by message, or by letter allegedly from us, as if the day of the Lord had already arrived. Let no one in any way deceive you; for the apostasy is to come first, and the man of sin is to be revealed, the one doomed to hell, the adversary who opposes and rises against every so-called god and what is worshiped, so that he seats himself in the temple of God with the claim that he himself is God." I Thessalonians 2:1-4.

It would be hard to put it more clearly than this. Simply said, the coming of Christ and our meeting together with Him will without question come after the apostasy occurs (falling away of nominal Christians) and the Antichrist is revealed and seats himself in the Temple. This event is the Abomination of Desolation and happens in the middle of the Tribulation, three and a half years after it begins, and three and a half years before Christ comes back. Paul had his pretribulation "prophets" to contend with just as we do today.

Daniel says,

"From the time when the daily offering is eliminated and the desolating abomination is set up there is 1,290 days (3 ½ years)**."** Daniel 12:11.

Paul tells us that the rapture will happen after this event, within 3 ½ years of Christ's coming. This places it absolutely within the last years of the Tribulation.

Paul again graces us with a specific time that the rapture will happen when he states in I Corinthians 15:51-52:

"Take notice; I am telling you a secret. We shall not all die but we shall all be changed, in a moment, in the twinkling of an eye, at the last trumpet call. For the trumpet will sound and the dead will be raised imperishable, and we shall be changed."

A last trumpet call presupposes that there are previous trumpets. It also means that there are no following trumpets. The seven trumpets of Revelation are the only series of trumpets described in prophetic Scripture. The seventh is the last of the series. At the seventh trumpet call, Christ's Kingdom is declared on earth; He has arrived, as Revelation describes it:

"The seventh angel blew his trumpet, and there were loud voices in heaven: "The kingdom of the world has become that of our Lord and of His Christ, and he shall reign forever and ever." Revelation 11:15.

Christ places the rapture at the end of the Tribulation

The weight of evidence really builds into a case beyond doubt when we see that Jesus Himself clearly places the rapture after the Tribulation:

"Right after the tribulation of those days the sun will be darkened and the moon will not shed her light; and the stars will fall from the sky and the forces of heaven will be shaken. Then will the sign of the Son of Man be shown in the sky, and all the tribes of the earth will mourn. And they will see the Son of Man coming on the clouds of heaven with great power and glory. And He will send out His angels with a loud trumpet call, and they will gather His chosen from the four winds, from one end of heaven to the other." Matthew 24:29-31.

We can see from these verses that the second coming and rapture clearly happen after the Tribulation and as both part of the second coming event. He also tells us that a shocked world will see both His sign and His coming. It will be anything but invisible. As Christ says, **"...with great power and glory."**

The exact day and hour, however, that the rapture occurs and Christ returns will be secret and unexpected. He admonishes everyone to be ready:

"Then there will be two men in the field - one will be taken and one left...Therefore you also be ready; for the Son of Man is coming at an hour when you do not expect Him." Matthew 24:40,44.

This admonition of readiness is given within the context of the Tribulation period. If the rapture happens before the Tribulation begins, there is nothing to be ready for. Believers would be caught up to meet Christ and instantly transformed whether they are ready or not. If believers are not ready for the Tribulation, they will not be ready to endure this extreme test and will be more likely to become the easy victims of deception and violence.

"By his scheming he shall make the treachery, which he applies, win out: proud of heart, he shall destroy the unsuspecting." Daniel 8:25.

Instead of being raptured before the Final Period, the vast majority of believers will be betrayed and suffer at the hands of those they might have once considered their allies. Believers who are aware and ready, will be able to endure that test in order to be caught up when Christ finally does appear.

The Lord does not give this phenomenally detailed account of the Tribulation in the Gospels and Revelation just to satisfy our curiosity. He gives it to us so that we, unlike the world, will know what is going to happen and will be prepared for it.

If the rapture is supposed to happen before the Tribulation, then Christ's teaching about the Tribulation, as well as most of the book of Revelation has little to do with Christians today beyond academic interest. There is little need to be concerned about it because believers will be safely and comfortably raptured away; but Christ makes it clear that Revelation is written to all the Church and,

"...he who has an ear let him hear what the Spirit says to the churches." Revelation 2:7.

In addition to all this evidence, Revelation gives us other clues to a posttribulation rapture. Christ tells the Philadelphia church that they will be spared the test that is coming upon the whole world. He gives the Loadicean church no such guarantee but instead emphasizes their need to be disciplined and tells them that He is at their door.

"The ones I love I correct and discipline; so burn with zeal and repent. Behold, I stand at the door and knock..." Revelation 3:19,20.

Just before the Tribulation begins the Spirit of Christ will be knocking at the door of the Church. Even among Evangelicals, most fellowships may be so stubbornly entrenched in extra scriptural doctrines that they will not even hear and will refuse to open the door. They will miss the opportunity to have a more close and honest experience with Christ that will be vital to enduring the test the coming days.

The divisions between each age of the seven churches usually come and go without any obvious or sudden changes, just as one generation of the world gives way to another without a discernible line to mark their passage; but they can be distinguished by their overall personalities. The age of the Philadelphia Church will come to an end when the Laodicean Church's distinctive personality emerges to replace it.

Following World War II, there was an explosion of growth in the Evangelical Church that continued for more than 50 years. A talented, enthusiastic group of young men and women spearheaded an evangelism and discipleship effort that spread out across the globe and personified the great age of the open door. These ministries are in their twilight, now, and their influence has largely been replaced by ministries that are more focused on self-improvement and "prosperity" than preaching the Cross of Christ and seriously training disciples.

In Revelation 14 we see the Lord on the clouds for the harvest of souls after the tribulation:

"Another angel came out of the temple, who shouted with a loud voice to the One seated on the cloud, 'Thrust in your scythe and reap, for the harvest time has come,

because the earth's harvest is overripe.' So the One seated on the cloud swung His scythe on the earth, and the earth was harvested." Revelation 14:16.

This cloud is the symbol of Christ's return. He now wears a crown and is in the act of returning for his saints, harvesting His own. Paul also describes this shout by the angel:

"For with a shout, with the voice of the archangel and the trumpet of God, the Lord Himself will descend from heaven, and those who died in Christ will rise first. Afterward we, the living who remain, will be caught up along with them to meet the Lord in the air." I Thessalonians 4: 16,17.

Another harvest follows shortly. An angel also has a sharp scythe:

"So the angel swung his scythe on the earth and gathered the fruit of the earth's grapevine, and threw it into the great wine press of God's wrath. Outside the city the winepress was trodden and blood flowed out of the wine press, so that for two hundred miles it come up to the horses bridles." Revelation 14:19-20.

These are two very different harvests. One is by Christ on a white cloud and the other is by an angel who gathers the world's grapes to throw them into the winepress of God's wrath. These are the two harvests at the close of the Tribulation. One describes the rapture and the other describes the immense slaughter of the world's armies as they attack Israel.

It is disturbing that a pretribulation rapture can become so entrenched among evangelical churches without Scripture to support it. This reflects the dangers of allowing major doctrines to be taught in churches and seminaries without insisting that they be being backed up by at least one clear verse of Scripture. Other false doctrines, like the separation of races, have also been taught within the Church with harmful results. Bigotry and sectarianism festered and spread when Christians took prevailing church teachings on race by blind faith instead of following the written Word. If one accepts everything one's church teaches without question, there is not doubt that one is going to be led astray at some point. Even the best churches teach things that are not correct. Check everything taught against the Word of God. Be a Berean or be deceived. (Acts 17:11). Christ commands us, **" ...allow no one to deceive you,"** not even popular Christian preachers, teachers, and self proclaimed prophets.

The last trumpet

The real rapture will happen at the last, the seventh trumpet sound. As the Apostle Paul writes, the dead in Christ will rise first, and then the remaining Christians who are alive will join Him in the air, instantly transformed into their glorious spiritual bodies. The world will be terrified and grieved because most will carry the mark of the Beast and know it is too late for them. They will realize that everything the Antichrist has been telling them is a lie. Like the wicked who were shut out of Noah's ark, there will be no salvation and no escape. They have no choice but to continue on their path to destruction. Even death will escape them. **"They will seek death without finding it."** This is a mystery: how people who wish to die, cannot. Anyone can easily take their own life, but some controlling power will keep the Beast's followers from committing suicide. Receiving the Mark of the Beast may lead directly to demonic possession. Even those who finally realize they are serving a Satanic power and are about to face the furious wrath of God, will be kept from harming themselves by the unclean spirits that possessed their bodies when received the mark of the Beast. The Mark may serve as an open invitation to any demonic spirit who is looking for a receptive body to posses.

"When an unclean spirit goes out of a person he roams through dry places looking for rest..." Matthew 12:43.

The demons that Jesus cast out of the man named Legion begged Him not to send them into the Abyss. When Satan falls to earth and opens this Abyss, he will have with him not only all the unclean spirits that have been thrown out of heaven, but also those he has let out of this great pit. During the last years of the Tribulation, these unleashed spirits will have an overwhelming influence on the world as they control the minds and bodies of the hoards that follow the Beast.

The Church will escape God's wrath

The Church will escape the direct wrath and judgment of God as the seven angels pour out the seven golden bowls on the kingdom of the beast. The vast stream of radiation and particles from supernova Arcturus that slam into our planet will wreck even greater destructions than the comet impact. Wormwood will only shake the earth, but Arcturus will shake even the heavens. It defies our imagination what it will really be like, certainly far from anything the planet has ever known.

"Behold, the day of the Lord comes! It is pitiless, accompanied with wrath and fierce anger, to make the earth desolation and to destroy its sinners out of it. For the stars of heaven and its constellations shall not give their light; the sun shall be dark at its rising and the moon shall not send out its light. I will punish the world for its evil and the wicked for their iniquity; I will put an end to the arrogance of the proud and lay low the boasting of the

violent. I will make mortal man scarcer than fine gold, and mankind rarer than the gold of Ophir. The heavens, therefore, shall tremble and the earth quake out of its place at the indignation of the Lord of hosts in the day of His fierce anger." Isaiah 13:4-13.

Born-again believers will not be caught in this final agony of our planet. A remnant of unbelieving Israel, however, will be, but at least 144,000 of them will be kept safe from the horrors and destruction just as Israel was during the plagues of Egypt, by God's mark on their forehead. Besides these 144,000, a remnant of Jews who resist the Mark will also manage live through this terrible period. They will eventually come to believe and will be gathered to await their Messiah, Christ Jesus, as the armies of the world led by the Antichrist invade Israel and surround them.

The ideal deception

If the hundreds of millions of born-again Christians suddenly disappeared today, almost everyone in the world would know what had happened and realize what they were saying was true. It would be impossible for any world power to deceive people about this. However, if the pretribulation rapture is a false doctrine, it will serve the purposes of the Antichrist ideally. If the Tribulation begins and the Antichrist makes his appearance with no rapture, those Churches that teach this will have to either deny what is taking place or admit that at least one of their major doctrines is wrong, making everything else they teach suspect. This will make it easy for the world to dismiss them. If the post-tribulation rapture remains a minority belief in the Church, it will be difficult at first to convince the Church that the Tribulation has already begun. This is exactly what Satan would want, for Christians to be unprepared and the world to remain oblivious to what is happening until it is too late.

As the rapture takes place at Christ's coming, the whole world will see it, but only the Jews who have resisted the Mark, will still have the chance to believe and be saved. The time of the Gentiles will be over. They will have missed their chance to repent. The rapture and visible, glorious Second Coming will be undeniable proof to the beleaguered Jewish nation that Jesus is the Messiah and their only hope.

The spectacular, glorious, worldwide event of Christ's return on the clouds will be visible to everyone on Earth. We are clearly warned against expecting a secret return

Chapter 16

Preparing for the Tribulation

There are two times in history when multitudes of people had the privilege of being at the right place at the right time to see the visible, awesome glory of God: the Jews who came out of Egypt with Moses, and everyone who witnessed the ministry of Jesus Christ. A third time will be for those who are on earth during the Tribulation and Second Coming. Imagine all the prophesies from Genesis to Revelation being fulfilled right before your eyes. Knowing exactly what is happening in that troubled time will be a great motivation to remain faithful and endure to the end. Knowing that Christ Himself will come back on the clouds within seven years to rescue His saints will give a deeper dimension to believers' lives that they have not had since the first century.

God does not consider time the way we do. As the Apostle Peter tells us, in his description of the Last Days,"**...with the Lord a day is as a thousand years and a thousand years as one day.**" II Peter 3:8. He can let a thousand years go by with hardly anything of great significance happening, such as in the middle ages, and then suddenly pack a phenomenal number of miraculous and important events into a few short years.

God is going to work wonderful things in the saint's lives in the midst of the greatest test humanity has ever seen. The Church will endure its greatest test ever, facing death rather than submitting to the Mark of the Beast. John describes how God will wipe away all tears from their eyes.

"For the Lamb, who is in the center of the throne, will shepherd them and will lead them to springs of living water. And God will wipe all tears from their eyes." Revelation 7:17.

The extreme suffering that will come upon the Church at this time will make it necessary for the Lord Himself to wipe their tears away.

Jesus warns His disciples about the persecutions of the last days:

"You will be betrayed by parents and brothers, by relatives and friends, and some of you will be executed. You will be hated by everyone for confessing Me... be on your guard, so that your hearts are not overloaded with dissipation, drunkenness and worldly cares, and that day takes you by surprise like a trap; for it will come upon all the inhabitants of the globe." Luke 21:16,17,34.

Those believers who are centered on worldly cares and selfish pursuits will be surprised like a trap, completely unprepared for the extreme test of the Tribulation.

The Church victorious

In Revelation 15 we see the Church now in heaven just before the bowls of wrath are poured out on the earth:

"And I saw something like a glassy sea mixed with fire, and those coming off victorious over the beast and over his statue and over the number corresponding to his name; I saw them standing on the sea of glass, holding the harps of God." Revelation 15:2.

The Church is described here as victorious even though

Revelation 12 says that the Beast was **"allowed to make war against them and to conquer them."** Why? Because, as 12:11 tells us,

"And they have conquered him (the dragon) **by means of the blood of the Lamb and by the world of their testimony; they have not loved their lives, even to the point of death."**

The Church's victory is a spiritual one. They will succeed in remaining steadfast in their faith and testimony even in the face of the most heinous persecutions ever. The blood of the Lamb is the means by which they will conquer, that is, extraordinary feats of courage and endurance will be inspired by the love of their Savior and the certain knowledge that He is soon coming for them. The Beast will eventually succeed in neutralizing the Church by brutal violence, but not before the Church demonstrates to Israel and the Jews an extraordinary faith and love inspired by the Cross of Christ.

Being unprepared is not an option

In the Gospels, Jesus warns us over and over again to be prepared for the trials of the Tribulation as well as His coming. He says, **"Remember that I have forewarned you"** (Matthew 24:25). It is our responsibility to be prepared after such a massive amount of prophesy about the last days has been graciously revealed us. It is clear that Christ wants His church to be ready. We have no excuse if we are not.

The preparation has to be both spiritual and strategic. Spiritually, just knowing what will take place will be a great advantage. This is why it is a great tragedy that a pretribulation rapture is being pushed in evangelical churches. Few of the believers who expect to be safely caught up before hand will be really ready for it. Besides the fact that they are inadvertently disobeying the Lord by not being ready as He commanded us, they will not have the advantage of being able to "hit the ground running" with the Gospel to a world whose trust in worldly answers will be violently shaken. The old stock answers to the world's problems will cease to be relevant in the context of the bloodiest warfare ever imagined. There will be a prevailing feeling even among nonbelievers that the end of the world is truly at hand. Those who are expectantly prepared are the ones who will be able to pass the test, remain faithful, and fulfill their purpose in the final days of history.

Becoming one

The Church will have to come together as never before. We will not have the luxury of being a hundred thousand different fellowships all working separately. Christ's commandment to love one another and become one will have to become a reality instead of just a pretty thing to say. A belief in a pretribulation rapture is one of the ways that the Church is becoming lukewarm, expecting to be cozily caught up without ever being put to the test.

An obsession with money and trendy self-improvement doctrines that are being widely taught in the Evangelical Church are creating a generation that is in desperate need of being purified. Nepotism is the rule of the day as important ministries are being turned over to ministers' children to keep successful pulpits and the money they generate in the family. It is obvious the Holy Spirit is being brushed aside in these important decisions. These second generation ministries are the beginnings of the Laodicean Church. The attitude has become, **"We are rich, we need nothing."** They will in turn be brushed aside as the Lord says in Revelation 3:16,

"So because you are lukewarm and neither hot nor cold I am going to spew you out of my mouth."

Christ warns some of the seven Churches that He will come and take their lamp stand away. This has happened repeatedly throughout history to churches and fellowships that have replaced the Gospel, the Word of God, and sound doctrine with the self-indulgent doctrines of worldliness.

Getting our spiritual lives in order is the most important way to prepare us for the great test ahead; standing on a firm foundation of sound doctrine, being clean vessels, and committing ourselves to wholly to Christ and His Kingdom. As Jesus commanded His disciples before their first great test at His crucifixion, **"Watch and pray,"** the Tribulation generation is exhorted to:

"...be vigilant and pray unceasingly so that you may have strength to escape all those impending events and to stand in the presence of the Son of Man." Luke 21:36.

Strategic planning

Strategic planning should also be done as the world moves closer and closer to the opening of the seven seals. When a hurricane is bearing down on a city, unbelievers and believes alike are wise to prepare for it. This storm of violence and evil will tear the fabric of the present world order apart. The institutions we rely on now will not protect us from the unprecedented troubles ahead.

The point of strategic preparation is not to hunker down in a basement somewhere and try to wait it out. The purpose is to remain a viable body of evangelistic Christians; as always, the light of the world and the salt of the earth, not a lamp hidden under a basket.

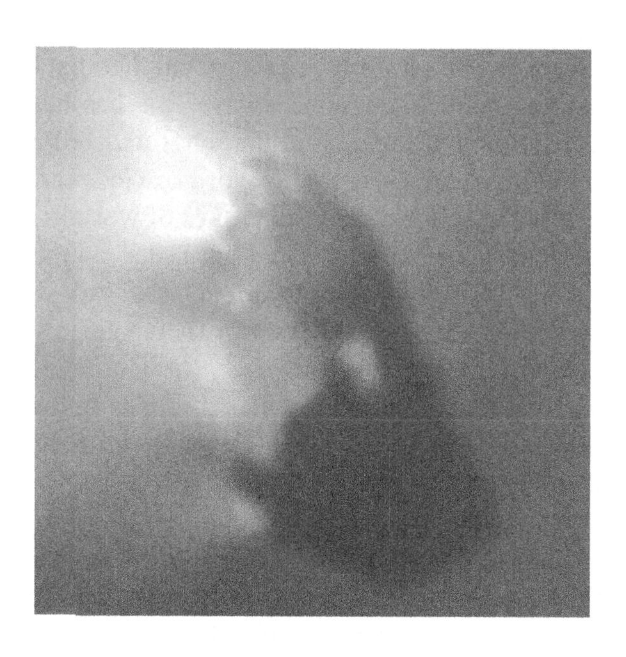

The turbulent head of Halley's Comet, taken by a passing spacecraft. The Church will have to prepare for the impact of a similar object from space. NASA

Stockpiling food

The first step in getting ready is to take the prophecies we have been given and do exactly what we should do in their light. Stocking food is the most obvious one. The bloody wars of the four horsemen will destroy the manufacturing and agricultural infrastructures of most countries. The third seal is famine. In many major conflicts more people die of famine and disease than from violence. Stocking up on food is simply taking God at His word. Since we know that the tribulation will last for seven years, a seven-year supply of food would seem wise. Food can be one of the most effective evangelism tools. What a testimony to unbelievers that a well-prepared Church would be to the reliability of God's Word and the life-changing power of Christ.

Where food is stocked is just as important as when. Those who want to go into the country and build a bunker and fill it full of food are probably the first ones who will have it taken away. Food cashing might be a more reasonable alternative. Being able to move around will probably be key to survival. Cashes of food in various places will facilitate movement from a place of danger to a safer one. Like a squirrel that buries his nuts various parts of the yard against the long winter, believers will be wise to do the same. The location of these cashes could also be shared with other Christians and Jews who are on the run from persecution.

Access to safe water will also be essential. Portable water filters and distillers would be indispensable.

Fuel, especially gasoline, will be at a premium, if available at all. Vehicles that run on alternative, homemade fuel, like methane, alcohol, and solar electricity could keep on running indefinitely.

Medical supplies and medical knowledge could mean life or death for many.

Self-defense will also have to be planned on. Although for Christians, using deadly force to protect lives may seem contradictory to turning the other cheek, the realities of a world whose order and institutions have failed, will leave it up to believers to protect themselves from marauding bandits and genocidal armies.

Communication and trade will have to continue in some form. A proprietary communication system will have to be set up to help the saints stay in contact with one another. An underground economy will have to also be instituted to usurp the economy of the beast and his mark.

An underground railroad of sorts, like that of the anti-slavery movement, will have to be built to help both Jews and Christians escape their persecutors.

The horrors of the Tribulation will be a boon to false religions and false prophets. Terrified people will be easy victims for every preaching egomaniac who sets themselves up as a voice of God, even as Christ Himself. Some false sects and cults are already preparing for the last days with stockpiles of food and supplies. Groups that do, will have an advantage over real Christians who do not, and will most likely see their numbers swell to lead millions into the false hopes of their authoritarian sects.

Flee to the mountains

In Matthew, Jesus warns his disciples that when they see the Abomination of Desolation occur, to flee to the mountains. The mountains and other rugged places will be the best places to survive. Living out on the plains somewhere, no matter how remote, would make anyone an easy victim. You only have to take a look at any successful guerilla campaign to see that their greatest ally is the rugged mountains, hills and forests used for a safe haven and an effective base of operation.

It is very difficult to say what will remain of the military infrastructures and equipment after the most deadly wars in history. Nuclear weapons will no doubt be used, at least to a certain extent. Certainly, there will be great destruction of most nations' armies and armories without much of a manufacturing base to replace it. Whether most satellite and computer networks will still be functional is questionable. Anyone who has access to either will have a great advantage. The destruction may be so complete that the armies that arise from the ashes may actually have to go back to horses and camels to help move personnel and supplies.

The beginning of the Tribulation will not likely mean a survivalist existence, but Christians may be able to live among the general population and share the Gospel. The first years will likely be a lot like World War II. As the years go by, though, the situation will grow more extreme until the Antichrist gains worldwide powers to launch an all-out persecution of Christians and religious Jews following the Abomination of Desolation.

There is no doubt that Bibles and Christian literature will be aggressively destroyed. This is where the spiritual conflict will heat up immensely, producing a final, fierce battle in heaven between Satan and Michael. Satan will be thrown out just before Wormwood impacts the planet. Millions of Christians will be martyred, and the Church as a functioning body of evangelizing believers may almost cease to exist. Even Christ wondered out loud, when He asked,

"When the Son of man comes, will he find (the) faith on earth?" Luke 18:8

Mere survival will probably be all that can be expected from these remaining saints in the last few years of the Tribulation who wait for the sign of the Son of Man and the appearance of Jesus Christ and His glorious resurrection/rapture. Their reward will be their bodily ascension into the heavens to meet their King, as Christ reveals,

"But he who perseveres to the end will be saved."Matthew 10:22

Not the salvation of the soul, which has already been accomplished, but the salvation of the body, from the experience of physical death. Paul said,

"I am telling you a secret, We shall not all die, but we shall all be changed." I Corinthians 15:51.

Desperate, desperate days

The Scriptures tell us over and over again that the horrific events of the Tribulation will be like none ever experienced in history. It will be well outside of human expectations, beyond our ability to prepare completely for it. Christ tells us very plainly that if God had not shortened those days, **"not a single person would survive."** If the Messiah does not come back and put an end to the destruction in time, humanity would come to complete extinction. The greatest miracle of that time may not be the pouring out of plagues on the earth, but stopping them. An Arcturus supernova will take an immense power to keep it from completely wiping out most life forms on the planet, including mankind.

So how do you protect yourself, your family, and your church from such horrific cosmic disasters? World War III is only the beginning. Believers will have to survive not only a bloody war but famine, disease, and the persecutions of the one-world government under the Antichrist, followed by a comet impact, as well as earthquakes, poisoned air, fires, and tsunamis. Believers will not have to be concerned about the effects of the explosion of Arcturus and the seven bowls of God's wrath because those events will take place after the rapture and second coming. Unbelievers only will suffer the catastrophes of the seven bowls. The 144,000 sealed Jews will be supernaturally protected from all the plagues by the mark on their forehead, just as the Jews were protected in Egypt during the Exodus.

Kingdoms of the cults

Sectarian factions that are obsessed with preaching about the last days are a great temptation to anyone who wants to study about these prophesies, but they teach law without grace, salvation by works instead of as a free gift of God through faith. Most are much harder to get out of than to get into. They keep their members hopelessly dependent on them by threatening the loss of salvation if they leave. They invariably claim some kind of exclusivity of knowledge, revelation, and authority. They are not only deceptive but they can be violent and dangerous as well. It is not uncommon for cults and authoritarian sects to subject their followers to all kinds of psychological, physical, and sexual abuse; sometimes going as far as murder and coerced suicide.

If any group denies the full divinity of Jesus Christ, salvation by faith in Him alone, as well as the new birth, they are one of the many false sects and cults that Christ Himself warned about and are to be carefully avoided. He tells us that you will know them by their fruit. A genuine, consistent Christ-like character should shine through. He rules our hearts with love, not with fear. The manipulative, legalistic, and authoritarian personalities of these sects eventually gives them away. They may hold a flower in one hand but they have chains in the other. Any organization that insists that they are the exclusive way to know God and be saved has set themselves up as the savior in place of Christ. Jesus Himself is the only way to know God and obtain salvation.

False prophets and false Christianity have been a serious problem from the very beginning of the Church, and will get even worse as the Tribulation gets under way. Insist on a doctrinal statement or a statement of faith when encountering a purportedly "Christian" group in person, on the Internet, or in publications. Many sects do not want you to know what they really teach.

Sadly, there are some evangelical groups that have degenerated into sect-like organizations. Legalistic fundamentalists or experience obsessed charismatic groups may describe themselves as the only true followers of Christ, or proclaim themselves filled with the Holy Spirit and exclusively anointed. These judgments belong to God. Bragging about them is arrogant and a sign of spiritual immaturity.

The Scriptures should always be the first and final word in all matters of truth, revelation, prophecy, and doctrine. Any such group that elevates any other writing, teaching, authority, or experience, as equal to or above the Word of God is certainly false.

Chapter 17

Armageddon

Most people who have only a casual knowledge of prophecy do not realize that the four horsemen of the Apocalypse and Armageddon are two different wars. The Tribulation will begin with one and end before the other; in between are all the horrors and persecutions brought on by the Beast, as well as the cosmic disasters that will shake the planet.

Armageddon is the last rampage of violence committed by the enemies of Christ after He returns to rapture His Church and save Israel from annihilation. Armageddon is the place where the armies of the world gather in Israel before they attack the remnant of Jews and their King.

The ancient city of Meddigo, which is under excavation in Israel today, lends its name to this final conflict of the age. The broad, cultivated valley that lies below the hilltop where Meddigo sits is also known as the Valley of Jezreel. The Beast will persuade or coerce the leaders of the world to muster their troops here.

As the Tribulation approaches its end, the Antichrist will finally control the political, military, and religious institutions of the world. The Church will have been decimated as Israel and Jerusalem suffer under the domination of the Beast. The vast majority of people in the world will carry the mark of the Beast and be firmly in his camp. There will be only one thing left on his agenda: to annihilate the remaining Jews and Christians who resist his mark and refuse to bow to his image.

The two witnesses

The two witnesses will be a thorn in the side of the Antichrist for the last three and a half years of the Tribulation. They have supernatural powers to shut up the skies to prevent rain and send plagues among their enemies. These men are God's final warning to an evil world that judgment is at hand. Most people will be beyond repentance, but there will surely be some who have not received the Mark and still have a chance to repent, receive Christ and be saved. The two witnesses are individuals, but they also represent Israel and the Church, God's two covenants and two testimonies to the world,

"The two olive trees and two lamps that are standing before the Lord of the earth." Revelation 11:4.

They are symbolic of the Church and Israel both working together during the Tribulation to give the world's inhabitants their last chance to repent and be saved. The Antichrist is finally allowed to kill these last two prophets. It is a day of rejoicing for the world and he feels he can move ahead with his final solution, but they rise from the dead after 3 ½ days and ascend into heaven at God's command to **"Come up here**." This is Revelation's version of the rapture and may preview the universal rapture of the Church by just a few days or weeks. The Beast's plan for Israel's annihilation is then ruined by the sudden appearance of the sign of the Son of Man and the arrival of Christ Himself.

There is a lot of speculation about who the two witnesses will be. The Apostle John may be one of them.

Shortly before these two are mentioned, John receives a little scroll to eat and is told,

"You must prophesy again about many peoples and nations and tongues and kings." Revelation 10:11.

There is also a mysterious comment made by Christ in the Gospel of John in which he tells Peter,

"If I want him (John) to remain until I come, what is that to you?" John 21:21.

We can gather from these incidents the possibility that the Apostle John never died and will return with the other witness, who may be Elijah himself. It is appropriate that one of the witnesses will be a Hebrew Prophet and the other an Apostle, one witness from the Church and one from Israel.

Arcturus pours out its plagues

"In that day there shall be no light; but cold and freezing. It will be a unique day known to the Lord, neither day nor night..." Zechariah 14:6.

The impact of the supernova will temporarily plunge the world into unnatural darkness, producing painful, super cold weather. The tremendous atmospheric disturbances will create a cloud cover over the planet and an artificial winter like none experienced in history.

An unprecedented massive earthquake will rumble around the globe as the effects of Arcturus strike the planet. It will be so universal and tremendous that every city in the world will be shaken to pieces, leveled. Even islands and mountains will be dislodged. Jerusalem will be broken into three parts. The worst nightmares of humanity will be fully realized. The world will be on the verge of total destruction, mankind facing extinction. Incredibly, Christ's appearance and these horrific plagues will not dissuade the Beast and his followers from attacking the remaining Jews in Israel. This will show Satan's absolute control over those who have received his mark. The Beast will send out three frog-like demons to all the armies of the world to force them to join him in Israel for the final war on the Jews and their Messiah.

Like Moses with the plagues of Egypt, Christ will pour out His judgment on the kingdom of the Beast. The aftereffects of Arcturus will hit the world as the last great battle of the age forms up at Armageddon and in the hills and valleys surrounding Jerusalem. One of the results of this catastrophic destruction by a nearby supernova will be that the Euphrates river will dry up, creating an invitation for the kings of the east to join the armies of the Beast. This eastern army has a 200 million man cavalry that kills one third of humanity, one and a half billion people by today's population count, as it moves across Asia, the middle east and into Israel.

Multitudes, multitudes in the Valley of Decision

There may be as many as two billion troops surrounding Jerusalem for this dramatic climax of history. This vast army will bring the livestock, food, clothing, gold, and supplies from the destroyed cities of the world with them. The countryside of Israel will contain much of the world's riches. A small remnant of Jews will face off this uncountable hoard of humanity. The Scriptures say that in the ensuing violence the blood will come up to the horse's bridles for almost 200 miles and mountains will melt from the blood.

As the nation of Israel repents and finally turns to Jesus as their Savior, they will weep for their Messiah. The realization that the One they have rejected for thousands of years is the only One who can save them will cause them immense grief. When Israel's stubborn heart is finally broken, their tears will flow like never before.

"...and they shall look on Him whom they have pierced; they shall wail for Him as one wails for an only son..." Zechariah 12:10.

"...even those who pierced Him will see Him..." Revelation 1:7.

Jerusalem's Golden Gate, waiting for Christ's return. Both Jews and Christians believe that the Messiah will come through this gate when He arrives. Muslims closed it up and put a cemetery in front to try to prevent this event

Satan may see this as his last opportunity to disprove the Scriptures, since God has always promised to restore and save Israel. If he can annihilate this last remnant with his vast army, he may feel that he has a chance to change his preordained fate. The death and destruction will be on an almost unimaginable scale.

Christ will destroy them, **"by the breath of His mouth."** The armies of the world will be struck with blindness and horrible decay, then viciously turn on one another. There is no real brotherhood in evil. Zecharaiah provides a graphic description of this judgment:

"...their flesh shall waste away while they are standing on their feet; their eyes shall fester in their sockets, and their tongues shall decay in their mouths...each one will grasp the hand of his neighbor; yet his hand will go up against his neighbor." Zechariah 14:12-13.

The armies of the world will cut each other to pieces. Those Jews who bravely face the armies of the world will stand victorious:

"In that day I will make the chiefs of Judah like a fire pot with wood and like a torch of fire in a row of fallen grain; they shall devour on the right and on the left all the peoples around them...the one who is feeble among them shall be like David, and the house of David like God, like the angel of the Lord before them. In that day I shall seek to exterminate all the nations that come up against Jerusalem." Zecharaiah 12:6.

Judgment in the Valley of Jehoshaphat

The world's armies will come into the valley of Jehoshaphat, believed by many to be the Kidron valley, southeast of Jerusalem's city walls. But the Great Rift Valley, containing the Jordan River and the Dead Sea is the more likely site of the Valley of Jehoshaphat. It is appropriate that this deepest of all the scars on the globe will be the site for the great judgment of the nations.

"Let the nations bestir themselves, and come up to the valley of Jehoshaphat; for there, will I, the Lord sit to

judge all the nations round about. Bring forth the sickle, for the harvest is ripe; go in and tread, for the wine press is full; the vats overflow, for the wickedness is great. Multitudes, multitudes in the valley of decision." Joel 3.

This judgment is not the final judgment of the world as individuals, (which will happen at the Great White Throne) but the judgment of the nations as political and national entities; the destruction of all worldly kingdoms by the King Himself. Revelation gives another description of this event:

"So the angel swung out his scythe on the earth and gathered the fruit of the earth's grapevines and threw it into the winepress of God's wrath. Outside the city the wine press was trodden and blood flowed out of the wine press, so that for two hundred miles it came up to the horses bridles." Revelation 14:19,20.

It is tempting to see this as just a symbolic exaggeration. Blood up to the horse's bridles for almost two hundred miles? Mountains melting in blood? With the coincidence of extreme weather phenomena together with the slaughter of possibly billions of combatants in the hills and valleys of Israel, a great slurry of water mixed with blood could cover vast areas of that small country, drain into the Great Rift Valley, actually turning it red with blood, chest-high for hundreds of miles.

"With pestilence and with blood I will enter into judgment with him, and I will pour upon him, upon his hoards, and upon all the nations in his train, floods of rain accompanied by hailstones, fire and brimstone..." Ezekiel 38:22.

Natural or supernatural?

The impact of a supernova explosion near our solar system may be the vehicle by which God pours out His final judgment on a murderous, satanic world. Even unbelieving skeptics can understand the immense destruction that a stellar disaster this close to the Earth would cause our planet. The plagues, the violent superstorms, the unprecedented earthquakes, and even the shaking of stars and planetary systems in our galactic neighborhood could certainly be caused by a force of nature, a supernova explosion of a nearby star.

God has created this vast universe to demonstrate His glory and serve His purposes, as well as to precisely execute the cosmic events of the Last Days. NASA

Some may think that the last seven plagues poured out on the Beast's kingdom will be completely miraculous, that it would be more glorious for God to just speak the words and bring them about instantaneously, instead of using a force of nature. He could certainly do this, but it is even a more awesome reality that He planned this day billions of years ago before He created the universe and set all the stars and galaxies in motion and timed them to perfectly fulfill all these ancient prophesies for the last days. There is nothing random and spontaneous about natural events, they are all under the Creator's control. The universe is not just a background for the events of history, it is the forge and the cradle He uses to shape them according to His unlimited power and perfect foreknowledge. Some of the seven bowls may, in fact, be instant, miraculous events; but most will certainly be a result of natural, cosmic phenomena much like those that have changed our planet in the past. Being ready, both spiritually and strategically, is the response that the Lord intended when He gave us such a rich bounty of revelation about the approaching final period. But no matter how prepared we are for it, it will be futile if we are not in a true relationship with Him as Savior. He has paid the price on the Cross for our salvation but each of us must individually accept that gift by faith and invite Him into our hearts to forgive us and give us the free gift of eternal life.

The time to receive Christ is now. This is the age of grace. Once the Tribulation begins the devious deceptions of the Beast and his prophet will make it nearly impossible for the average person to discern what is real and what is not.

Chapter 18

The Coming One

The Lion of Judah roars

The great mystery of the ages of who God really is and who His people are, will be suddenly reveled to every person on the planet. No one will be able to deny it and Satan will no longer be able to hide it. Both the resurrection/rapture and the appearance of Christ on the clouds will make it perfectly clear to every human who has received the mark of the Beast that they are about to come under the judgment of God.

"Then the kings of the earth and the nobles, the generals, the wealthy, the powerful, yes everyone, slave and free, hid themselves in the caves and in the mountain rocks, and called to the mountain rocks, "Fall on us and hide us from the presence of the One who is seated on the throne, and from the wrath of the Lamb, for the great day of their wrath has come, and who is able to stand?" Revelation 6:15,16.

Major events of the Second Coming

The exact order of events of Christ's return following the Tribulation can be difficult to decipher. The sequence may unfold something like this:

1. SIGN OF THE SON OF MAN IS SHOWN IN THE SKY:

"Then will the sign of the Son of Man be shown in the sky, and all the tribes of the world will mourn." Matthew 24:30.

2. CHRIST APPEARS ON THE CLOUDS:
"And they will see the Son of Man coming on the clouds of heaven with great power and glory." Matthew 24:30.

3. RESURRECTION AND RAPTURE OF THE CHURCH:
"And He will send out His angels with a loud trumpet call, and they will gather His chosen from the four winds, from one end of heaven to the other." Matthew 24:31.

4. CHRIST DESCENDS TO THE MT OF OLIVES:
"This Jesus, who was taken up...will come again in the same manner..." Acts 1:11.
"His feet shall stand in that day upon the Mount of Olives..." Zechariah 14:4.

5. WEDDING OF CHRIST AND THE CHURCH IN HEAVEN:
"...the wedding banquet of the Lamb has come and His bride has gotten Herself ready." Revelation 19:7.

6. THE 7 BOWLS OF GOD'S WRATH ARE POURED OUT:
"And I heard a loud voice from the temple say to the seven angels, 'Go your way and pour out on the earth the seven bowls of God's wrath.'" Revelation 16:1.

7. DESTRUCTION OF THE NEW ROMAN EMPIRE:
"She is fallen, fallen Babylon the great! ...For in a single hour she has been laid waste." Revelation 18:2,19.

8. ARMIES OF THE WORLD GATHER AT ARMAGEDDON:
"They go out to the kings of the whole earth to muster

them for the war of the Sovereign God's great day...So they mustered them at the place called in Hebrew, Armageddon." Revelation 16:14,16.

9. CHRIST REAPPEARS ON A WHITE HORSE:
"God comes from Teman, the Holy One from Mount Paran...Thou dost march out for the deliverance of Thy people." Habakkuk 3:3,13.
"Then I saw heaven open and a white horse appeared. Its rider is called Faithful and True; justly He judges and wages war." Revelation 19:11.

10. BATTLE OF BOZRAH IN EDOM (southwest Jordan):
"Who is this who comes from Edom, with crimson-stained apparel from Bozrah?... 'I have trodden the winepress alone.'" Isaiah 63:1,3.
"Then the Lord shall appear above them...the Lord God shall give a blast on the ram's horn, and He shall move in the tempest of the south...The Lord their God shall save them in that day like the flock of His people..." Zechariah 9:14,16.
"The Lord shall save the tents of Judah first..." Zechariah 12:7.

11. CHRIST LEADS ISRAEL INTO JERUSALEM:
"A highway shall be there (in Edom), **yes, a way; it shall be called the Holy Way...The ransomed of the Lord shall return and come to Zion with singing and everlasting joy..."** Isaiah 35:7,10.
"...then I will take you, one of a city, and two of a family, and I will bring you to Zion." Jeremiah 3:14.

12. BATTLE OF JERUSALEM:
"In that day the Lord shall defend the inhabitants of Jerusalem...In that day I shall seek to exterminate all the

nations that come up against Jerusalem." Zechariah 12:8,9.

13. JUDGMENT IN THE VALLEY OF JEHOSHAPHAT:
"Let the nations bestir themselves, and come up to the valley of Jehoshaphat; for there, will I, the Lord , sit to judge all the nations round about." Joel 3:12.

14. CHRIST ESTABLISHES HIS MILLENNIAL KINGDOM ON EARTH:
"In that day they shall call Jerusalem the throne of the Lord, and all nations will be gathered to it..." Jeremiah 3:17.
"Blessed and holy is he who shares in the first resurrection. Over them the second death exerts no power; instead, they will be priests of God and of Christ, and will reign with Him a thousand years." Revelation 20:6.

We can see clearly from the Scriptures that the Second Coming of Christ is not a single, simple event but has multiple theaters that include the Church, Israel, and all the nations of the world. Other events that deal specifically with many of the countries that surround Israel such as Egypt, Syria, Moab (Jordan), and Babylon (Iraq) are detailed in the Scriptures as well.

Scenario for the Day of the Lord

The Great Tribulation comes to abrupt end as the sign of the Son of Man appears in the heavens and Jesus comes on the clouds for the entire world to see. The saints, living and dead rise to meet Him in the air, instantly transformed into their spiritual bodies. He then descends to the Mount of Olives in Jerusalem, which splits into a great valley. The beleaguered Jews in Jerusalem flee through this valley and across the Jordan River, and out into the wilderness.

Christ may then return to heaven to wed His Church.

In the meantime, Satan compels the armies of the world to mass into the Middle East to destroy Israel once and for all. It may appear that God has abandoned the Jews as they take refuge at Bozrah. The golden bowls of God's wrath are then poured out onto the earth. The shock wave of Arcturus slams into the planet, causing unimaginable devastation to the world and the kingdom of the Beast. The New Roman Empire falls and little is left of the western countries of Europe and America.

The Jews are protected from the plagues of the seven golden bowls of wrath by the seal of God on their foreheads. The tribe of Judah gathers in the wilderness of Edom at Bozrah, while the 144,000, the restored twelve tribes of Israel, wait for their King on Mt Zion in Jerusalem.

As the armies of the world close in on the Jewish remnant, Israel as a nation finally calls out to Jesus to save them. At Mt. Sinai, He appears again, this time on a white horse with all the saints and heavenly armies with Him. Quickly, furiously, and completely He destroys the attackers surrounding Bozrah. He then leads Israel north up the Kings Highway, across the Jordan River, and into Jerusalem. The armies of the world surround Jerusalem and flood into the Great Rift Valley to cut off the returning Israelis. They are confronted by the One who treads the winepress of God's wrath. Over the hills and valleys of Israel, up the Jordan Valley, and into the Valley of Jezreel the conquering King pursues the followers of the Beast, striking them with blindness. They turn on one another and cut each other to pieces. The Great Rift Valley flows chest high with blood for almost 200 miles.

Satan, the Beast, and the Prophet are seized and thrown into the Abyss. Christ enters Jerusalem through the eastern gate, establishes His throne in Jerusalem, and begins His thousand-year reign on earth.

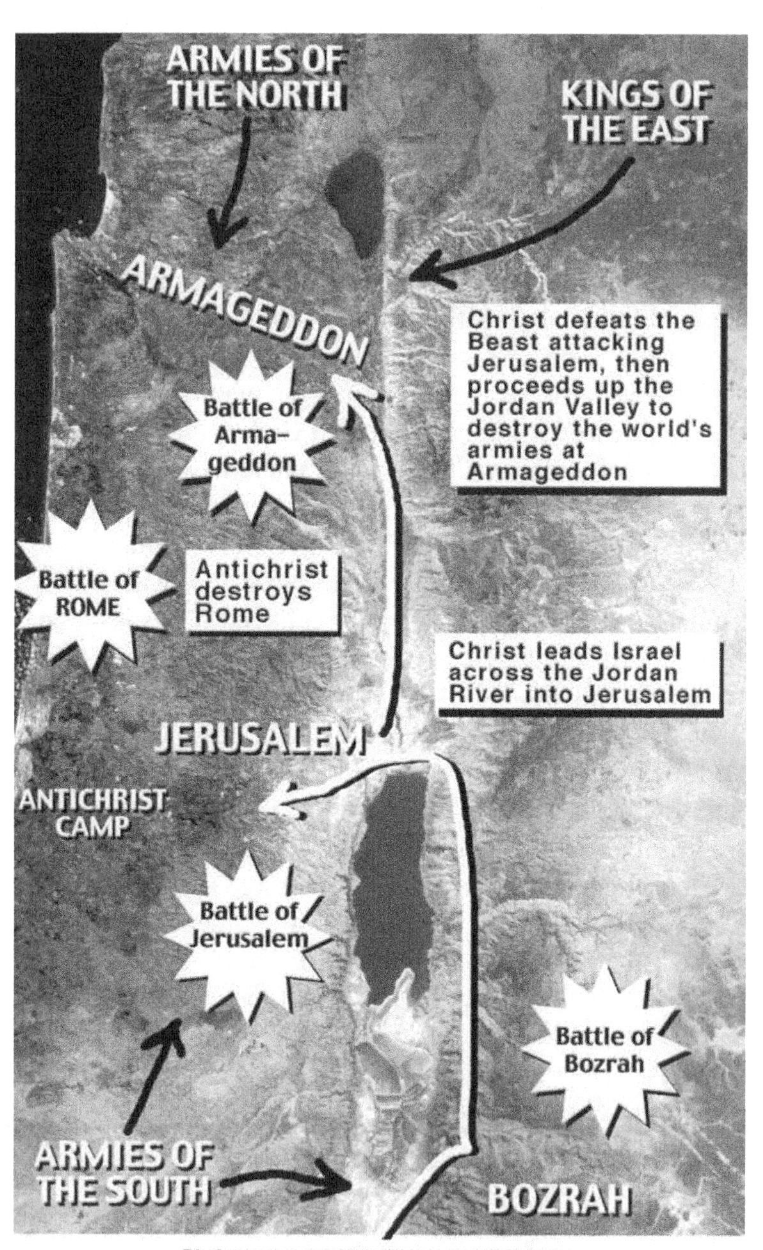

Christ returns at Mt Sinai and destroys the armies surrounding Israel at Bozrah

All of the governments, religions, philosophies, sciences, and schemes of mankind have never been able to bring peace and justice to the world. The Prince of Peace will do it suddenly, completely, and wonderfully when He returns.

"The sun and moon are darkened, and the stars withhold their shining. For the Lord roars from Zion, and from Jerusalem He utters his voice. The heavens and the earth are shaken; but the Lord is a refuge for His people and a stronghold for the sons of Israel." Joel 3:15,16

Chapter 19

The Shroud and the Supernova

The Shroud of Turin, it seems, would not have anything to do with heavenly signs. This enigmatic strip of cloth has been both disparaged by skeptics and passionately defended by those who believe it is not only the burial cloth of Jesus, and holds an actual image of Him, but is physical proof that He rose from the dead. Curiously, a cosmic event - a supernova, may prove to hold the key to the true date of the Shroud.

In 1974 a team of scientists were allowed to study the Shroud, taking samples from it and putting it through as many rigorous tests as was possible at the time. Based almost exclusively on the carbon-14 dating of the Shroud material, the scientific community concluded that it was a 13th or 14th century fake. No one, however, has been able to establish how the image was made, where the blood and DNA found on the cloth came from, or how someone in the 14th century could have created a photographic negative 500 years before the invention of photography! The image on this piece of cloth has proven to be the most puzzling mystery of any single artifact in history.

How could the perfect anatomy and impeccable forensic details of the Shroud have been produced during an age when there was no one around with the skill and knowledge to accomplish something that can't even be duplicated today? How could pollen found in Jerusalem but not in Europe have ended up on a piece cloth that supposedly has never left Europe? How could an image using modern radar imaging techniques produce a striking, eerie, 3D sculpture of the man on the cloth when any other painting or photograph treated by the same techniques produces only a flat, distorted picture? How could this photorealistic image suddenly appear during the early Renaissance when there had never been anything this accurate until the invention of photography? The best efforts of the most talented painters of the Renaissance produce images that always betray the painter's artistic style. Even Da Vinci, who lived much later than the 14th century, created anatomical drawings and paintings that are easily identified by his style and techniques; and none could be confused with being a photograph. Why would an artist in the 14th century try to create a photographic negative when no one at that time even knew what a photograph was, let alone a negative of a photograph? A fraud would not have to go to such pains to produce something that no one at the time could understand or appreciate.

The Shroud of Turin would have been massively over-engineered for its purported purpose of counterfeiting a religious relic for some church or aristocrat. It demonstrates a sophistication of technique and understanding of science and forensics that has even stumped expert teams of modern scientist trying to figure out how it was made. An artist who could have somehow produced the Shroud would have been playing to an audience that wasn't there. Even the most educated people of the time would not have understood or appreciated all the unique, extremely sophisticated details present in the Shroud. We have to remember that a 14th century con man could not have had us in mind when he supposedly made this. He had only to fool his contemporaries, not 21st century scientific experts.

The face on the Shroud of Turin. All the powers of modern science have not been able to duplicate an artifact like this or even explain how it was made. You may be looking at a true image of Christ. Courtesy of the Archdiocese of Turin.

Carbon 14 comes from Supernovas

Since the Shroud of Turin was first clearly mentioned

in historical records in the 14th century, this date would seem to be a good match to the corroborating evidence of the carbon-14 date that also places it in the late 1200's to the early 1300's. There are problems with carbon-14 dating, though. Carbon-14 comes from cosmic radiation, mostly from distant galactic and extra-galactic supernova explosions. It has always been assumed that the carbon-14 in the earth's atmosphere has been at the same levels throughout human history. This would have to be absolutely true to make carbon-14 dating always reliable.

The Shroud is made of linen, a fabric that comes from flax, a plant grown to make cloth. When a plant dies the amount of carbon-14 that it has absorbed from the atmosphere begins to decay at a predictable rate. Since all plant material is believed to have the same percentage of absorbed carbon-14 while growing, the amount that an organic substance has left, compared with the amount of the ordinary, non-radioactive carbon present, can be used to calculate how old the material is. Carbon 14 dating is usually reliable, but far from infallible. There are some things that can skew the results, sometimes by thousands of years.

When scientists found unusually elevated carbon-14 levels in stalagmites in an underwater cave in the Bahamas, they showed that carbon-14 levels in the atmosphere have not always stayed the same, but could be subject to events that can raise these levels at certain times. A near-earth supernova explosion was suspected of raising the carbon 14 levels in the cave's formations.

If the flax of the Shroud was growing when one of these events occurred, it might have absorbed elevated levels of carbon-14, making it test much younger that it actually was, invalidating the results completely.

When could this spike have happened? If the plants the Shroud was woven from were growing at the time that the Bethlehem star came on the scene, this conceivably could have produced such a spike. If the Bethlehem star was some type of near-earth supernova, its brief flood of radiation might have caused a temporary elevation of carbon-14 that was absorbed by flax plants growing at the beginning of the first century and preserved in the Shroud of Turin.

If a scenario like this actually did occur, there is a beautiful irony to this story of a relic of Christ's death and resurrection being preserved as an article of faith, instead of a scientific certainty. The star of Bethlehem might have not only announced the birth of the Christ but also affected how the world today views the Shroud of Turin: as either a scientific impossibility or a reality taken by faith but supported by historical evidence. The Apostle Paul tells us that it is to the glory of God to keep His footsteps a mystery:

"O the depth of the wealth, the wisdom, and the knowledge of God! How inscrutable are His judgments and how untraceable His footsteps!" Romans 11:33.

Why?

"For judgment I have come into this world, so that the sightless may see, and those who see may become blind." John 9:39.

A vast amount of inexplicable evidence

The image in the Shroud of Turin (the non blood areas) is not caused by an added substance like paint, but is made by a physical change in the fibers of the cloth itself. The fibers in the image have fundamentally changed compared to the non-image areas. It is possible that initially there was no image on the cloth at all, but as the Shroud aged, an image appeared as the stressed areas turned a darker color. The areas with the bloodstains contain no image under them, indicating they were there before the image was created.

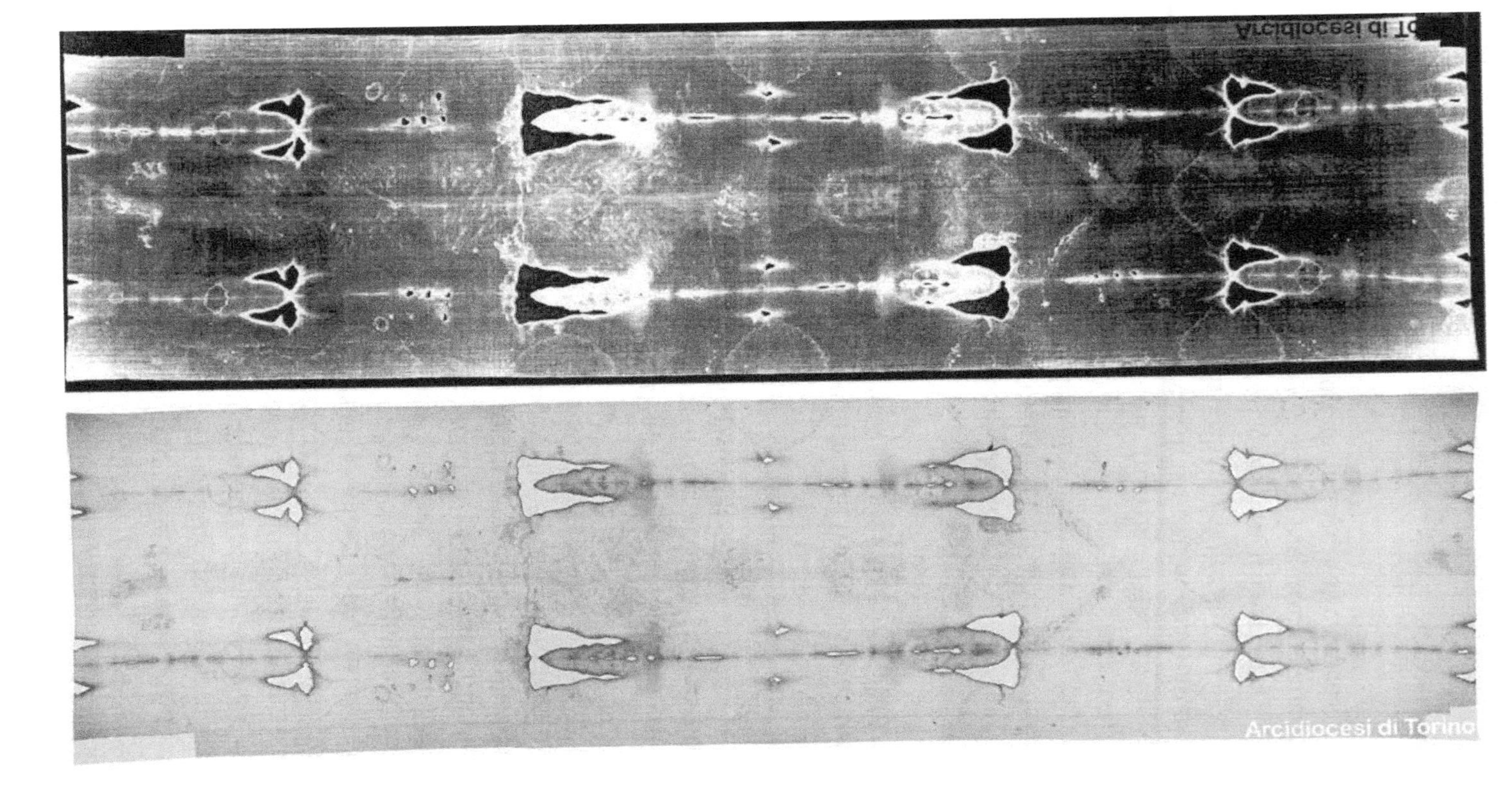
Arcidiocesi di Torino

Previous page: Original (left) and negative image (right) of the Shroud. The original image is really a negative image, and a negative of the original produces a positive image. Skeptical scientists date it to about the 14th century, over 500 years before the invention of photography. Courtesy of the Archdiocese of Turin

As one of the artifacts of the death and resurrection of Christ that the disciples would have been in possession of, the Shroud would have likely been saved as a relic; but the disciples might have been unaware that it contained a latent image of Christ. The faint image may have gradually appeared over the years to be finally noticed centuries later as the stressed image areas turned color. When it was photographed for the first time, the clear picture of the crucified man jumped out of the negative image, revealing itself as a positive image of the negative one that was there on the Shroud all along. No artists could have possibly anticipated the invention of photography 500 years later to reveal the perfect, positive image hidden there for centuries. The natural image on the Shroud is very faint, making it difficult to discern distinct features, but the photographic negative of the image is amazing, even shocking, in the details that it reveals.

Artists today can produce photorealistic paintings simply by taking a photograph and copying it centimeter by centimeter. Pre-photography artists had to create everything directly from life or another artist's work. Ten different artists painting the same thing will always create ten very different renderings reflecting their individual skills, style, techniques, and perceptive abilities. Even the best pre-photography artists painstakingly trying to create a painting that looked exactly like the subject could never produce works that we would mistake for a photograph. And remember, it is not just a photorealistic image, but also a negative photorealistic image, something that would be virtually impossible for anyone to create without a negative image to copy. This would be completely unnecessary and unknown to anyone before the invention of photography in the 19th century.

Another important point is the difference between the blood image areas and the body image areas. They are produced in completely different ways. The blood areas show up as if a liquid has come into contact with the cloth. They seep into the fibers. The body image areas do not, but change only the top layer of fibers with no seepage into the cloth. Why go to this all trouble? Why not just paint the entire image on?

If photography could not have been imagined or anticipated in the 14th century, then the physics of radiation certainly could not. If you hold the dial of a flourescent watch against a sheet of photographic paper and develop it, it will leave a ghostly image. The image on the Shroud has similar earmarks of such a radiation-imprinted picture. The map-like 3D rendering that radar imaging techniques produce could only result if the body itself was the source of the radiation. The parts of the body closer to the linen "film", such as the nose, would have to be a correspondingly lighter shade to create such a striking 3D topographical effect. An outside light source falling on a body cannot produce a 3D image using these techniques. The person who purportedly created the Shroud would have to know about this, again showing a comprehensive understanding of chemistry, physics, and photography that were nonexistent until well into late the 19th and early 20th centuries.

Other evidence that indicates the Shroud of Turin may be authentic is:

1. The subject looks right. It is a historically accurate image of a Jewish-looking man who was crucified.
2. The trauma that the body suffered exactly matches the details given in the Gospels that Jesus suffered, even down to

the shape and spacing of the barbell weights on the ends of the whip cords the Romans used at the time. Both cheeks show trauma as if from being slapped or beaten. The right side of the head shows massive swelling, evidence of a face that must have been grossly disfigured at one time. The side wound is apparent.

3. The signs of crucifixion contradict the traditional way Christ's crucifixion was depicted in art up to that time. The nail holes are in the wrists instead of the hands. The wounds on the head show that a hat of thorns covered the entire top of the head instead of just a band of thorns around the forehead as popularly depicted in paintings and sculptures.

4. The entire body is covered with whip wounds from head to toe, seldom depicted in crucifixion art. There is hardly a square inch of the body that has not been beaten or cut.

5. The back of the body is imaged with the same exacting detail as the front, a completely unnecessary effort on behalf of any artist. Again the anatomy and forensics of the back image are impeccable.

6. The subject has a ponytail. A style that 1st century Jewish men wore. A detail a 14th century artist probably would not have known about.

7. Dirt was discovered where the heel is on the Shroud, consistent with the makeup of the soil of Jerusalem.

8. The thumbs are hidden, turned underneath the palms, as would happen if nails were driven into the wrists; something not many people even today, except a forensic pathologist, would understand.

19. The format of the Shroud is unheard of in historical art and artifacts. The idea of a complete image, front and back, head to head is very original as well as completely unnecessary for any work contrived simply to be displayed as a relic.

10. Blood serum that has separated out of whole blood fluoresces under ultraviolet light. The blood areas on the

Shroud are surrounded by a narrow band that fluoresces, proving that the stains contain real blood in which the serum has separated out.

What is not there is just as important:
1. Special imaging techniques reveal that there is absolutely no brush or application pattern to the image as would always be the case of an artist brushed or applied some paint or substance to the cloth. The image is completely random.
2. There is no suspending paint media like oil on the shroud that would be there if an artist applied a liquid paint to the cloth to make the image.
3. The image has shown no tendency to run where water was poured on it to put out the fire during the 15th century. A pigment would run if water were poured onto it. The image shows no scorching in the areas where it was burned. If paint or some other foreign substance were there it would have scorched where it was painted. This shows that the image is present as a constituent of the cloth fibers themselves and not as an applied foreign substance.
4. There are theories that the Shroud is actually created by making a large photographic print but there are no silver compounds or any other chemical residues on it that would make this possible. No known photographic technique used even today can duplicate all the unique aspects of the Shroud image.

Photography is a complicated optical and chemical process that took scientifically sophisticated inventors of the 19th century decades to create. If photography was invented in the 14th century, just for this artifact, why is there absolutely no mention of its existence until the 19th century, and how could this be the one and only photograph ever made for more than five centuries? Silver compounds in photographs produce a black image. The negative image on the Shroud is a yellow-orange color. Even the photographs that have been produced to mimic the Shroud all have significant differences, like their inability to produce the three-dimensional information present in the Shroud.

This book is not about the Shroud but the fact that it's scientifically accepted dating relies almost exclusively on an understanding of supernova radiation brings it into the arena of this discussion. It is possible for a reasonable person to change from being almost sure that the Shroud is just another fake relic to believing that the Shroud of Turin may actually be a photographic image of Jesus Christ. The more the matter is investigated, the more it becomes obvious that the image on this piece of cloth doesn't come from the 14th century. It violates all the principals of science and historical knowledge that we rely on to classify an artifact of that period.

A very unscientific rush to judgment

The fact that it has been brushed aside so quickly by the scientific community says more about personal prejudices than the objective weight of physical evidence.

The rush to judgment on the Shroud of Turin by skeptics is not necessarily a bad thing. The idolatry associated with the Shroud would no doubt get out of hand if it were indisputedly determined to be a genuine 1st century burial cloth. As Paul said, the righteous will live by their faith. Faith in Christ is what saves us and makes us righteous before God, not overwhelming physical proof. The Lord gives us just enough historical evidence to require us to still take that step of faith that leads to salvation. Physical evidence does not persuade us trust God. Remember that Christ Himself performed miracles right in front of His detractors and they still wanted to kill Him. The pride and prejudice of the human heart is the greatest obstacle to faith, not lack of evidence.

We may yet see the Shroud of Turin play a role in the events of the last days. Believers have long been on the defensive because of the wide acceptance of Darwin's theory and scientific evidence that the universe appears to be billions of years old. In spite of the massive efforts by Darwinists and atheists to discredit the written Word of God, scholarly believers have been given enough of their own physical and historical evidence to effectively challenge this avalanche of hostile prejudices. Archeology and astrophysics, along with the pathetic failure of humanist philosophies to provide any solutions to the mankind's horrible problems (in fact making them much worse), have enabled Christians to confidently participate in the arena of fair and logical debate about the origins and purposes of mankind and the universe. Every day there is more evidence that the model the Scriptures give us of how the universe came to be is the only one that accurately describes the cosmos as well as the realities of the human condition.

The life of Jesus Christ, and all the other events of the Scriptures are presented as literal, historical fact by those chosen to bear witness to them and write the books we call the Bible. That is why Christians do not fear the truth of the physical sciences. They are confident that genuinely objective, unprejudiced research will eventually agree with everything written in God's Word.

Believers do not need physical evidence to prove that the Scriptures are historical, reliable and true; that is obvious by the way that the Spirit of Christ can change the human heart as no one else or nothing else can. The purpose of archeological, scientific, and historical evidence is to illuminate the ancient world that the Prophets and Apostles describe for a better understanding of the Scriptures themselves. Historical and archeological investigation also serves to expose the deceitful dogmas, petty hatreds, and personal prejudices of those who are underhandedly working to destroy Judeo-Christian values and beliefs for the sake of their self-serving social and political agendas.

History is littered with the bones of prejudiced philosophies that predicted the demise of the Christian faith. It is Darwinism, humanism, false religion, and anti-Christian prejudices that will all disappear when Christ makes His appearance on the planet once again.

"...you saw a stone, hewn without hands from a mountain, strike the image on its feet of iron and clay, breaking them to pieces... But the stone that struck the image became a great mountain and filled the whole earth." Daniel 2:34-35.

Chapter 20

The Millennium

When the smoke clears and judgment in the Valley of Jehoshaphat is over, what will the world be like? Who will be left on the earth when Christ begins His millennial reign? The fact is, that most of the world's population will have been killed during the Tribulation. If you are alive when the Tribulation begins, the chances are overwhelming that you will have less than seven years to live. So much death and destruction will take place, in fact, that the majority of survivors will probably be Jewish. The remaining unbelieving Gentiles may be those who have managed to hide themselves in remote places and escape being drafted into the armies of the Antichrist, carry his mark, and worship his statue. Most Gentile survivors may be children.

Planet Earth will be almost uninhabitable. The Scriptures tell of a great stench that will permeate the world from all the rotting corpses.

"For the Lord's anger is against all nations and [His] indignation against all their hosts; He has doomed them and has given them over for slaughter. Their slain shall be cast out; the stench of their corpses shall rise... " Isaiah 34:2.

The changes in the earth's atmosphere, geology, and

weather will make human life very difficult, if not almost impossible. Again, the Scriptures say, **"If those days were not shortened, not a single person would survive."** The destruction has the potential to wipe out every person living in the world.

When Christ begins His millennial reign in Jerusalem after Armageddon, His first task may be to set the planet back in order, but He will do it gloriously. The planet will become like heaven on earth, as He rules with absolute authority. There will be no such thing as war or tyranny. Israel and Jerusalem will be everything that God promised through the Prophets thousands of years ago. The great millennial Temple of Ezekiel will be built in Jerusalem. Peace will reign over the planet. The universe will witness what it will be like when God truly rules the world.

"In the latter days the mountain of the Lord's house shall be established as the highest of the mountains; it shall be raised above the hills, and the nations shall come and say, "Come, let us go up to the mountain of the Lord, to the house of the God of Jacob, so he may teach us His ways, and we may walk in His paths." Michah 4:1.

"The Lord will become King over all the earth in that day..." Zecharaiah 14:9.

"At that time they shall call Jerusalem the throne of the Lord, and all nations will be gathered to it, in the name of the Lord to Jerusalem." Jeremiah 3 14.

Many wonder who will repopulate the planet when Christ restores Israel and rules the world. The judgment of God will fall on the lawless, the wicked, and the followers of the Beast. Those people will be annihilated but many others who survive the Tribulation will likely be spared the fate of the wicked and will be given a chance to live on earth during the glorious Millennial reign.

Satan will be chained and thrown into the abyss for a thousand years. The world will be a strange mixture of physical and spiritual beings dwelling together. Believers, with their new bodies, will govern with Christ, being rewarded as mayors and governors. The Apostles will set on 12 thrones judging the twelve tribes of Israel. It may be a time of unimaginable progress and prosperity. The devastated world's population will recover and the nations of the world will bring their riches to Jerusalem to worship at the Temple there. Many of the Temple rituals will be restored with Jesus being the high priest and the very Presence of God in Jerusalem. A river of water will flow out of the Temple into the Dead Sea, turning it into a fresh water lake. Jews will be honored as especially revered citizens. People will live much longer than today, probably hundreds of years. Many of the problems that have plagued humanity since ancient times will be solved. Most diseases and medical problems may be eradicated.

The sin nature of the human heart, though, will not have been eradicated. The rebellious nature of man will still dwell within many, waiting to rise up and throw off God's rule. Satan will be released after a thousand years and will once more lead the nations into a last and final treachery of violence and rebellion. The forces of evil will once more rise up and attack the Millennial Kingdom of God but will be quickly defeated and the universe will never see conflict again.

The Great White Throne

The first resurrection described by John is the resurrection of the saints at the coming of Christ.

"Blessed and holy is he who shares in the first

resurrection. Over them the second death exerts no power; instead they will be priests of God and of Christ and will reign with Him a thousand years." Revelation 20:6.

All the other dead will not come to life until the end of the ages, at the Great White Throne Judgment. Every soul that ever lived on the planet will stand before God there to receive the final, eternal judgment on their life. This final judgment will start with a separation of the sheep from the goats, the believers in Christ from those who have not believed in Him. The books will be opened, and the most important one, the Book of Life will be opened. Every name recorded there will receive eternal life and will spend eternity in heaven with God. Jesus told His disciples,

"However, do not rejoice because the spirits submit to you, but rejoice that your names are registered in heaven." Matthew 10:20.

Every name not found in the Book of Life will receive punishment for every sin, secret and public; they have ever committed, and will be forever cast out from the presence of God.

True spirituality is not a smorgasbord of choices, to accept or reject as one feels, any more that the physical sciences are a matter of personal choice. Truth is truth, whether in the spiritual realm or in the physical. No one has the luxury to choose which laws of science they wish to obey to live in this world. We all must adhere to the same truths that govern the universe or pay the price for ignoring them. The spiritual principals that govern our relationship with our Creator are universal as well, absolutely the same for each one of us. The greatest deception in the world today insists that all spiritual paths are equally valid.

Christ's death on the cross provided the only way to know God and gain eternal life. Only the blood of Christ can wash away sins. There is but one truth and one way to be saved from the wrath to come.

"I am the way, the truth, and the life, no one comes to the Father but by Me." John 14:6.

Chapter 21

The Great Harlot

The destruction of the Great Harlot, the Babylon of Revelation 18, is given a great deal of attention in the John's Apocalypse. Clearly Rome, it rides on the back of the beast with ten heads. Arrogant, violent, and hedonistic, she is sure of her security and stature, but is destroyed in a single day by her own allies, led by the Beast. Described as the one who sits on many waters, today the Great Harlot takes the form of the Western Civilization, the countries of Europe and the Americas that grew out of the Old Roman Empire. The Roman Empire is believed by most to have fallen fifteen hundred years ago, but it has never really passed away. In fact we are still in the age of Rome, if you will, and our civilization is a continuation of that powerful civilization.

When Constantine became Emperor in the 4th century, he did two things that changed the Roman Empire into what it is today: he married it to the Christian church, and then took it out ofRome to Constantinople, creating what eventually became known as the Holy Roman Empire, Christendom, and eventually, Western Civilization. The statue of the book of Daniel that represents the five great empire/civilizations that would each in turn dominate the world until the end, has legs of iron but feet of both iron and clay. The iron legs are the Old Roman Empire; the feet of iron and clay are the New Roman Empire, the marriage of Greco-Roman culture to Judeo-Christian beliefs.

Constantine, the Roman emperor who mixed the iron and clay of the empire/civilization destined for destruction at Christ's return

It must be remembered that Daniel was written to Israel, not to the Church. The age of the Gentiles and of the Church is foreshortened. As any photographer or artist knows, foreshortening displays only what is visible from a specific perspective and excludes everything in between. The feet of iron and clay are the last small portion of the stature and refer only to the last 7 years of Israel's allotted time to prepare itself for the Messianic Age.

The Church age is invisible within the 70 weeks of Daniel, but a clue is given to its existence by separating the last week of years and placing it by itself. The two millenniums of the Gentile Church is what separates this last week. For the first time in history Biblical values and beliefs have become part of the fabric of the dominant civilization. Greco-Roman civilization has progressed and evolved; at times nakedly rising to the surface as its old self in imperial ambitions like Napoleon's and Hitler's, but has had to reluctantly temper itself with the high moral sense of Judeo-Christian ethics. As Daniel observed, iron and clay do not mix. Christianity and Romanism can coexist, but never really become one.

The Great Harlot rides upon the Beast with ten heads. Out of the destruction of the first wars will rise the new world order of the ten nations and upon them, the New Roman Empire. This new Rome will be an attempt to bring peace and security through a new PAX ROMA, a Roman peace by means of a centralized government and military in Europe and the Americas. The Antichrist has different plans, though. He wants a world empire; a world totalitarian state ruled by him alone as Stalin ruled the Soviet Union; with a bloody iron fist and total control over every mind.

Fiery end for the Great Harlot

In a desperate attempt to bring peace to the world, the ten kingdoms will surreptitiously hand their power over to the Beast, likely in the form of the world's nuclear arsenals. When he achieves this, he will scheme to remove the only obstacle to his totalitarian power, the New Rome. The Scriptures tell us that this Harlot who, "sits on many waters," (indicating that it is an empire or civilization that spans oceans) will be ravaged by plagues, then destroyed by a fiery conflagration in a single day. The most likely fulfillment of this prophesy is that the ten nations will hand over control of their remaining nuclear arsenals to the Beast, who will then turn around and unleash it on what is left of the cities and military institutions of the New Rome, creating a nuclear conflagration that will wipe out Christendom, the civilization that Constantine created 1,700 years ago.

Revelation gives a eulogy of this fall of Western Civilization, the civilization that has given the world its concepts of democracy, personal freedom, and scientific study, along with Judeo-Christian beliefs and ideals, but a civilization that has also instigated the persecution and murder of so many Christians and Jews over the centuries. The western societies' increasing hostility for toward Evangelical Christianity as well as for the state of Israel, along with its growing contempt for innocent human life, will bring this final judgment down upon it.

The underhanded, sneaky, and deceptive maneuvering of the world dictator will betray the world's expectations of personal freedom and religious liberty by snuffing out, once and for all, the world's institutions of freedom.

Even today, political groups within western countries are aggressively working to destroy the foundations that freedom is built on, the value of the individual and God-given human rights that come from Judeo-Christian beliefs. Without these, the world descends into a very dark abyss where individual human life has little value and the government becomes god, answerable to no one.

The Antichrist, with the help of his prophet, will take the last, final step that Satan desires and erect a statue of himself that all must worship. Satan tried to tempt Jesus to fall down and worship him by offering Him all the kingdoms of the world. Satan's ultimate goal is to coerce the world into falling down and worshiping him, believers and unbelievers alike. He will offer the false promise of eternal life to those who will, and death to those who will not.

Chapter 22

Predicting the day

Predicting the day that the Tribulation begins or the day Christ returns has proved to be a stumbling block for false prophets. Authoritarian sects and cults are notorious for setting dates for the last days that inevitably prove false. It is comical to watch self-appointed apostles dance around afterward trying to keep their money machines from disintegrating and their burned followers from abandoning them. Their usual strategy is to proclaim that it was really an invisible "spiritual" fulfillment. The self-deceptive nature of the human mind is truly amazing. Confronted with overwhelming evidence that they are being duped and led astray, many stubbornly follow falsehood right into the grave. More than anything, this shows how powerfully Satan can blind the minds of those who reject the person of Christ for the sake of some self-righteous religion:

"You investigate the Scriptures because you suppose that in them you have eternal life in them, and yet they bear witness to Me, yet you do not want to come to Me in order to have life." John 5:39.

Zealous religion without rebirth in the Holy Spirit can be an extremely destructive and dangerous thing.

"...the hour is coming when whoever kills you will think

that he is rendering service to God." John 16:2.

Without personally receiving Christ as Savior and being born of His Spirit, religion is just another way to be deceived and used by ambitious, manipulating charlatans. The true Body of Christ does not depend on a charismatic personality or an authoritarian structure to be unified in beliefs and mission. It is cohesive through the message of the Gospel and the true presence of the Holy Spirit, while tolerating distinctive teachings and practices concerning minor doctrines.

Evangelicals have made their own mistakes concerning date setting to confess. Whenever eschatology becomes popular in the church from time to time there is the inevitable predictions that Christ's coming is going to happen very soon, in a certain year, or on a certain date. When prophesy became the subject on everyone's lips in the 1970's many prominent ministers agreed that Christ would come in the 1980's, because it was a generation after the founding of the state of Israel. The millennium became another date that many evangelicals pointed to as the probable time of the rapture and Christ's appearance. The exploding Pentecostal movement has brought a hoard of self-proclaimed prophets predicting the time of the second coming as well as other events of the Apocalypse. Some ministers link almost every event in the news to something in Revelation or Daniel. While this makes for interesting and profitable programs, it serves no one but themselves and casts a shadow of illegitimacy that the entire body of believers has to bear.

A false prophet on every street corner

There are two events that will happen without anyone (except God) predicting the exact day and hour: the beginning of the Tribulation and the day that Christ returns. These are the two "bookends" of the Tribulation, and both are going to remain secret until the day, hour, and minute they occur. Anyone claiming to know either date is certainly a false prophet. Although the "season" these events will take place will be obvious to believers who are familiar with the prophesies of the last days. They may be predictable to within weeks of them happening. The greatest error for most believers will be their ignorance of the fact that the Tribulation has already begun. There will be no doubt about the return of Christ, because it will be visible to the whole world, although many will be led astray into believing that the Second Coming is a secret one and has taken place before it actually does. The Tribulation will be a time of vast deception, not only from the Antichrist, but from the thousands of false prophets and false messiahs that will spring up to take advantage of people's fears.

"If someone tells you, 'Look! Here is the Christ!' or, 'There He is!' do not believe him; for false messiahs and false prophets will arise and show great signs and wonders to mislead, if possible, even the elect. Remember that I have forewarned you. So, if they say to you, 'He is there in the desert,' do not go out; 'In these rooms here,' do not believe it. For like the lightning flashes from the east and is seen in the west, so will the coming of the Son of Man be. Wherever there is a corpse the vultures will flock there." Matthew 24:23-27.

These charlatans will attract followers like a corpse attracts vultures, the self-glorifying deceiving the self-righteous; hordes of people convinced their religion will save them instead of a personal faith in Christ and rebirth through the Holy Spirit.

Matthew's generational eras

Still, there may be clues in the Scriptures for the

approximate date of the Tribulation and Second Coming. Matthew divides Israel's history into three periods of 14 generations: from Abraham to David, from David to the Babylonian exile, and the Babylonian exile to Christ. Abraham to David is about one thousand years. From David to the Babylonian exile is about 500 years, and the Babylonian exile to Christ is about 500 years. Matthew skips some individuals in his genealogy, showing that he is dealing with generation averages, not exact numbers.

Fourteen generations of 36 years is 504 years. If you add four more periods of 504 years to the first three periods of 14 generations, presuming Christ was born in 4 BC, that would add up to 7 periods ending in 2012. The end of each 14 generational period marks a major turning point in God's dealings with His people. Because there are 7 eras of 14 generations and 7 is the number of God's completed plan, 2012 or somewhere near that date could well turn out to be the next turning point. Whether this means the second coming or the beginning of the Tribulation is another question to consider. If it means the Second Coming, then the Tribulation would start seven years earlier, which would be somewhere around the year 2005.

This theory is based on an interpretation that Matthew's generational eras can be projected into the future, which may or may not be a legitimate presumption. It also assumes that 504 years closely defines 14 generations, which may or may not be accurate either; it may be more of an average than an exact period.

It all depends, as well, on the date of Christ's birth, which is not precisely known. The birth of Christ could have happened anywhere from 5 BC (before Herod the Great's death) to 6 AD (the date of the census mentioned in the Gospel of Luke). If Christ were born in 6 AD, this would push this estimate back to 2022.

The world and Israel

The state of affairs between Israel and the world is deteriorating rapidly. Anti-Israel and anti-Jewish sentiment is spreading across the globe even among nations that have had little contact with the Jews or Israel. The tide is clearly turning against them without legitimate reason. The worldwide sympathy they enjoyed following the holocaust of World War II has largely evaporated.

When the whole world reaches the point of being set both against Israel and the Gospel, then the nations of the world have put themselves under a curse and under God's judgment. The Tribulation will follow shortly.

The United States will likely be the last nation to support Israel, but with the way political winds blow in this country, it will not take much for an extremist government to come to power that refuses to support Israel. The 2000 presidential election was almost a dead heat. It should have been an easy win for conservatives after the moral scandals of the previous presidency, but the left wing's "government-is-god" mentality has become almost as prevalent in American society as it has in Europe. The continuing moral decay and twisted world view of a humanist culture that is increasing hostile to Judeo-Christian ideals and beliefs, will guarantee that an extreme government will be come into power in the US within the next generation.

The political left seems to have all but abandoned Israel, in favor of the Arab-Islamic expansion, rejecting the Jewish people's right to the land they lived in for thousands of years. This is a strange alliance; the socialist, agnostic left on the same side as violently zealous Islamics. A shared hatred for Judaism and Christianity seems make comrades out of natural enemies in the same way Herod and Pilate struck up a friendship following their treachery against the Lord.

Chapter 23

Doorway to the Third Heaven

The Apostle Paul mysteriously mentions that,

"I know a man in Christ who fourteen years ago - whether in the body or out of the body I do no know, God knows - was caught up as far as the third heaven."II Corinthians 12:2.

Paul was surely talking about himself and the source of his phenomenal understanding of Christ and the Gospel. In Revelation, John is also invited to enter the door into heaven where God is enthroned. The account of his experience there describes what the realities of the spiritual universe looked like to this 1st century man. These realities are the vital source of the events that will happen to the world in the last days of history. The third heaven is a place that is almost beyond the ability for anyone, especially someone living during the age of Rome, to translate. John uses rare gemstones to describe the color and substance of much of what he saw there. The beauty and wonder must be beyond what we can imagine even today.

There are three heavens. The first is the physical universe where the laws of physics apply. The second is the spiritual heavens, where the Holy Spirit, Satan, angels, demons, and the souls of people travel about and interact with the physical universe. The third heaven is the throne room of God Himself, the heavenly Temple of which the Mosaic Tabernacle, Solomon's Temple, and Herod's Temple were crude representations.

When Christ tells us that the heavens as well as the earth will be shaken, the point is, that the realities of the spiritual realm, even of God's Heavenly Temple, will change dramatically and this change will be reflected in the shaking of the heavens and the earth. The universe is not just a great mass of space and time that is floating about randomly on it's own. It is designed, created, and sustained by the Word of God to fulfill a specific purpose and perform on queue according to God's intricate, preordained plan.

In the Great Throne Room, the universe expresses itself in the form of the four living beings. These are not just symbolic representations, but real beings or persons, who inhabit this third heaven. They are a type of cherubim who are inspired by the overwhelming glories of God to constantly praise Him:

"Around the throne, on each side, there were four living beings full of eyes in front and behind; the first living being was like a lion, the second, like an ox, the third with a man-like face, and the fourth, like a flying eagle. Each of the four living beings had six wings, and each living being was full of eyes all around and within. Neither by day nor by night do they cease saying, 'Holy, holy, holy, Lord God Almighty, who was, and who is, and who is coming." Revelation 4:6-8.

They represent the four aspects of God's creation; the lion may be the untamed universe, the ox: the tamed universe, the man: humanity, and the eagle: the spiritual universe. The eyes they have all over and within expresses the presence of the Holy Spirit that sustains the universe and revels their purpose: to be a witness to the power and glory of God. Their wings are their abilities, but the number six suggests their imperfection and incompleteness, just as in itself, the universe is imperfect and incomplete.

In Romans, Paul describes the creation almost as if it were a person, capable of emotions.

"For the creation eagerly awaits the revealing of the sons of God; for the creation was subjected to frustration, not from choice but from Him who effected that bondage, and that with hope; because the creation itself will be liberated from its enslavement to decay into the glorious freedom of God's children. For we know that to this day the entire creation has been groaning and suffering agony together as if in childbirth." Romans 8:19-23.

Even astronomers have discovered that the universe is on a one way trip to oblivion. It has a limited life span just as any life form does. The universe is expanding and decaying, and its fate, if left alone, is for every star to burn its fuel and eventually blink out, ending in a dark, cold cosmos. Light in the natural universe would cease to exist. The physical universe is waiting for its redemption from this decay at Christ's coming, but its agony will accelerate as the Tribulation deepens.

The four living being take part in the events of the Tribulation. As mentioned before, they hand the seven angels the seven golden bowls of God's wrath. The universe has been designed over billions of years to come to a point to conspire with God's plan on that day to pour out its destruction on the kingdom of the Beast and announce Christ's return. A supernova explosion at exactly the right time and the right place may be one of the four living beings' contributions to Christ's confrontation with the world's vast armies that are poised to annihilate Israel.

Israel from Space. The Holy Land will go through some amazing transformations during the Last Days. The whole land mass will rise, making Jerusalem the highest mountain. The Mt of Olives will be split by a great valley. A spring will flow from the Temple and into the Dead Sea, turning it into a freshwater lake. The desert will become a lush, Eden-like garden. NASA

Watch for previews

In the coming years we can expect to see more things on earth and in the heavens that preview what will take place after the Lamb opens the first of the seven seals. In our lifetime we have seen the most violent event to occur in our solar system possibly since the dawn of civilization, the impact of Shoemaker-Levy on Jupiter, one of our neighboring planets. That massive world, thousands of times the size of the earth, swallowed the fragmented comet up without any apparent damage to its permanent structure or appearance. Our planet will not be so fortunate.

Twenty-four elders, the seven torches, the burning alter, the Father on His throne, and the Lamb also show themselves in this vision of the Third Heaven. Magnificent angels make their appearance as well, to round out this awesome drama. If one of God's purposes is to put on a great show, this will be the greatest, and those in heaven will have the best seats. The believers on earth will have to endure the persecutions and plagues, keeping faith that their deliverance is near.

The twenty-four elders are the representatives of Israel and the Church, the twelve Patriarchs and twelve Apostles; the fruit that Christ's sacrifice has borne from mankind. The altar before the throne is God's justice and righteous judgment. The seven torches are the seven Spirits of God, the Spirit of the Creator in His complete, encompassing perfection.

Jesus stands there also as the Lamb that was slain; with seven eyes as the perfect expression of the Spirit of God, and seven horns to perfectly assume the Father's authority.

Christ holds the seven angels of the seven churches as a constellation of stars in His right hand. These seven angels, no doubt, are also the seven angels that play the major roles throughout the events of the Final Period.

The incense that rises before the Throne are the prayers of the saints. This is the presence in heaven of every believer who comes before the Throne of the Almighty in prayer. God does not just hear our prayers, but has preordained that they play a vital role in the great events that will culminate in Christ's return.

Chapter 24

Loadicea - Our Lukewarm Church

Only two of the seven churches of Revelation are commended without being criticized by Christ: Smyrna and Philadelphia; the persecuted church and the church of the open door. Persecuted churches and churches enthusiastically engaged in evangelism have a focus and commitment to Christ and the Gospel that keeps them on track. Churches that are not, usually find themselves losing their way. The last church of the age, the Laodiceans, are so lukewarm that the Lord says that He will spit them out of His mouth. As a matter of fact, He would prefer that they were cold rather than lukewarm. Someone who has strayed completely has the potential to be convicted of their sin, leading to grief and repentance, as Christ said,

"But the person who is forgiven little, loves little," Luke 7:47.

The door of the Laodicean Church is closed so that even Jesus must knock to get in. The days of the open door Church of Philadelphia are over as nation after nation outlaws the preaching of the Gospel. The days of easy evangelism may soon come to an end. Preaching Christ will mean persecution, imprisonment, and even death for Christians around the world.

The Church can achieve deeper spiritually and greater

fruit in times of difficulty and danger than in times of comfort and prosperity. Many believers that have lived in the lap of luxury most of their lives see no reason to pursue deeper and more genuine doctrine and discipleship. Maintaining the status quo has become the primary objective for the rich, lukewarm churches of this Laodicean age.

Buying gold

"Buy from Me gold that has been tested by fire," Christ tells the Laodiceans, **"The ones I love, I correct and discipline, so burn with zeal and repent."** Revelation 3: 18,19.

The church is going to be disciplined as never before. Self-indulgent teachings will not stand the test. The Tribulation will destroy those ministries that are not ready for it. They will be spit out, uprooted, broken off, and replaced by ministries that are ready and willing to meet the challenges of the final period.

It is interesting to note that believers who have gone through severe persecutions seem more willing to accept the fact that the church may have to endure the Tribulation. The ministries that seem to be most vehemently opposed to this teaching seem to be those that are rich, comfortable, and successful. Self-improvement and prosperity has replaced the message of the Cross and sacrificial discipleship on the preaching agendas of many evangelical ministries. It is no longer what you can do for God, only what God can do for you. Living for Christ and His Kingdom has taken a back seat to the individual's selfish agenda. Buying gold tested by fire means listening to those who have truly been through fire and have something of deeper substance to teach the church. The wood, hay, and stubble of wealthy, lukewarm churches will be cremated in the crucible of the Apocalypse.

The challenge is great but the rewards are greater

Christ will have a special relationship with the Tribulation church, as He does with all persecuted believers.

"For the Lamb will shepherd them and will lead them to springs of living water. And God will wipe away all tears from their eyes." Revelation 7:17.

The Lord never forgets those who have given all for Him.

Of all the rewards promised to the seven churches, the one promised to the Laodicean saints who remain faithful seems to be the best:

"As for the victor, I shall grant him to sit beside Me on My throne, as I also conquered and sat down beside My Father on His throne," Revelation 3:21.

"These are the ones who have come out of the great Tribulation, and they have washed their robes and made them white in the blood of the Lamb. For this reason they are before God's throne, and day and night they serve Him in His temple, while He who sits on the throne spreads His tent over them." Revelation 7:15.

Stumbled, but not fallen

Daniel revels that,

"On the part of some teachers their stumbling shall be for their refinement and purification to make them white, preparatory to the final period." Daniel 11:35.

When the Tribulation begins, the evangelical church will no doubt be shocked, many in denial, and some ministries ruined. Others will be able to admit they were wrong and face the test with faith and courage. Those believers and ministries who know they will not be comfortably taken away in a pretribulation rapture will be ready to resist the deceptions and persecutions and fulfill their purpose of being a witness to and protector for the Jews and Israel. Many will be more receptive to the message of Christ in the face of such worldwide destruction. It is tribulation, more than prosperity, that makes believers Christ-like.

"You rejoice in this, although now for a little while, if it must be, you are distressed by various trials, to that the testing of your faith, far more precious than perishable gold that is tested by fire, may prove to be for praise and glory and honor when Jesus Christ is revealed." I Peter 1:6,7.

The stumbling of the church is not to its ruin, but to purify and prepare it for the final day when the Sign of the Son of Man will flash over the planet to announce that the Messiah has returned.

Science catches up to the Scripture

The prophet Daniel asks God,

"To what outcome does it all run?" God answers, **"Move on, Daniel, for the words are secret and sealed until the final period."** Daniel 12.

The accumulated knowledge we have of the mechanics of the universe may be part of the clearer understanding that is promised to believers in that final period. The detailed descriptions that Christ, the Prophets, and the Apostles give of the spectacular cosmic events that will take place have just recently been illuminated by the growing body of knowledge in astronomy and astrophysics. We are entering and age where science's agreement with the

Scripture is getting harder to ignore, so much so as to make the atheists and agnostics that dominate scientific institutions a little nervous. Anti-deist and anti-Christian philosophies are crumbling before the weight of evidence coming from the scientific community itself that the Earth was created as an extremely unique place in a universe that is otherwise absolutely hostile to life. The search for life outside of our planet has produced nothing. Still, the belief in extraterrestrials has become like the official religion of many academic and scientific groups, who seem desperate to find something to disprove the Scriptures. This obsession to denigrate the Bible seems to be the supreme motivation of so many in the academic and scientific communities.

Chapter 25

When the Fig Tree Finally Buds

Jerusalem Fig Tree

"Learn a lesson from the fig tree. As soon as her branch becomes tender and puts out leaves, you know that summer is near. When you observe all these things, you know that He is so near, that He is at the door." Matthew 24:32.

The Lord is specifically talking about the Tribulation here but in order for the Tribulation to begin, certain events and conditions must be in place throughout the world to set it up. Some of these are:

1. Alignment of all nations against the Gospel of Christ
2. Alignment of all nations against Israel
3. Worldwide persecution of Evangelicals and Jews
4. Worldwide obsession with Jerusalem
5. The appearance of a charismatic world leader intent on unifying all political, philosophical, and religious camps
6. The completion of the Great Commission: the Gospel preached to all the world
7. Changing alliances and a destabilized world order
8. Widespread religious trends that promote spiritualism, occultism, paganism, and satanism
9. A prevailing political movement that promotes a one-world government/religion
10. An unusually great number of sects promoting false prophets and false messiahs
11. Prevailing character of an entire generation that is cold, selfish, mean, dishonest, violent, greedy, and hedonistic; in short, wicked
12. A serious effort to build a Temple in Jerusalem

These are signs that the world is approaching critical mass by aligning itself in absolute opposition to Christ. It is clear that the unbelieving world is fast approaching a state of intransigent unrepentance. Just as God turned to the Gentiles when Israel rejected His Son, so will He give the Jewish Nation another chance when the Gentile world rejects Christ and His Gospel, seeks the destruction of Israel, and begins to set up a one-world government.

The great mysteries of the last days

Many things written in the Scriptures about the last days have remained a mystery in spite of all the study by sincere believers throughout the centuries. God is the Lord of surprises. It is impossible for anyone to predict everything He will do and exactly how He will do it as He fulfills His plan of bringing history, as we know it, to an end. He has given us a great deal of clear, detailed revelation to inform and guide us through this time, but many things will be unexpected even for learned believers. To be sure, Christ will return, the saints will be resurrected and raptured, and Israel will be saved; the Antichrist will arise to deceive the world, and the armies of the nations will be judged and destroyed. Many details and specifics of how these events will unfold are yet to be understood by even the most gifted prophesy students.

When Jesus presented Himself to Israel, He was soundly rejected by many of the most expert religious scholars of the time. Their fatal flaw was not in their scholarship or intellect, but in their hearts. Jesus Christ was both much more and much less than they ever expected of the Messiah. They were not looking for the Creator Himself to come into their midst; One who could forgive sins, answer prayer, raise the dead, and call God His own Father.

They also failed to grasp the duality of the Messianic prophesies, and the fact that before God sent them the Messiah as their conquering King, it was necessary for Him to first send Him as the Lamb, to pay the price for the world's sins once and for all time. So too it will be as the Tribulation begins. No one will be absolutely sure about how everything will unfold. Those who claim such ability are surely false teachers. The Scriptures hint at some of the surprises yet to come. The Apostles had received insights to many of the details of the last days that are lost to history. In his second letter to the Thessalonians, Paul mentions that he had explained some these details to them while with them, but does not tell us exactly what they were. We can only guess.

Coming soon

"Behold a white horse, and He who sits upon it is faithful and true." Revelation 19:11.

Christ is the central figure of the Apocalypse. Even though the Antichrist forces himself on the world, it is the Coming One who has foretold it all and is ready to reveal Himself to the world once again. We see Christ in three roles in John's Apocalypse: as the Lamb that was slain, as the One who comes on the clouds, and as the King on the white horse.

Today Christ is the Lamb, tomorrow He will come on the cloud to gather His saints, and finally, He will come back to rescue Israel, judge the nations, and establish His Kingdom on earth.

When Jesus appears on the clouds, all believers, living and dead, will rise to meet Him in the air. The Church will then stand before the Throne in heaven. It will be time for the wedding of the Lamb. The bride will be ready, dressed in the white linen of her righteous deeds. The conquering King will then reappear on His white horse, his robe dipped in blood as He treads the winepress of God's furious wrath. His victory at Armageddon will become the feast of the wedding banquet.

He holds the keys

It is important to note that the great evangelistic book of the Bible, the Gospel of John, has little to say about the prophesies of the last days. The point being, that the focus of any study of God's Word should first of all begin with the person of Christ; His life, teaching, death and resurrection. A personal relationship with the Son of God is primary to everything else we can learn from the Scriptures. He is wisdom, righteousness, power, and salvation incarnate. His

Spirit alone can give the sincere student of prophecy a clear understanding about what they read.

The Cross of Christ leaves its eternal mark in every book of the Bible. The prophetic Scriptures are no exception. As John witnesses the Son of God in his heavenly glory, He reminds us:

"I am the First and the Last and the Living One. I experienced death and behold, I am alive forever and ever, and I possess the keys of death and its realm." Revelation 1:17,18.

It was He who began history and it is He who will bring it to an end. Christ alone holds the keys to our future and to each of our lives. Get ready, the Brilliant Morning Star is coming.